The Commentary
to Mishnah Aboth

Moses Maimonides

The Commentary
to
Mishnah Aboth

Translated, with an Introduction and Notes,

AND A TRANSLATION OF MISHNAH ABOTH BY

ARTHUR DAVID, D.H.L.

*107
M1*

BLOCH PUBLISHING COMPANY
New York

To my wife Mildred,
and to our dear children,
Miriam and Jonathan

Foreword

ALTHOUGH it will surely be inadequate, a word of gratitude is due my teachers. It was my good fortune to be introduced to the world of Moses Maimonides by Professor Shalom Spiegel, Professor of Medieval Hebrew Literature at The Jewish Theological Seminary of America. Beyond his being an eloquent and inspiring teacher, his never-failing kindness serves as a constant source of encouragement. I was privileged to write my doctoral dissertation under the guidance of Professor Salo W. Baron, Professor Emeritus of Jewish History, Literature, and Institutions, at Columbia University. His patience and modesty are matched only by his wisdom and learning. Professors Boaz Cohen, Abraham J. Heschel, and Abraham S. Halkin of The Jewish Theological Seminary of America, have always been generous in granting me the favor of their cooperation.

The manuscript was read by Dr. Ben Zion Bokser, Rabbi of The Forest Hills Jewish Center. His learned comments and observations were of considerable value.

It goes without saying that all errors of any nature are mine and not his. May he be granted strength and length of years to be able to be of assistance to others. I wish to express my sincere thanks to Mr. Phillip Ritzenberg who edited the manuscript, and to Mrs. Gertrude Serata who assisted me in my library work.

Only the members of a loving family would permit their father to deprive them of many hours which rightfully should have been theirs. Throughout the entire preparation of this book, my wife Mildred, and our dear children, Miriam and Jonathan, were patient and kind to the extreme of excess.

Contents

Introduction

THE Rabbinic tradition regards the Torah that Moses received at Sinai as the complete revelation of God's will. Implicit in the words of the Torah is the course for man to follow. Although its precepts in their explicit form did not chart the path of proper conduct for all conditions of life, the Rabbis believed that the diligent study of the Torah would reveal it. Accordingly, they developed the concept of the Oral Tradition. The Written Torah, or the Written Tradition, was viewed as the basic blueprint of the Divine purpose. The Oral Torah, or the Oral Tradition, represented the amplification of its spirit and intent. Both traditions served to establish the Halachah, the right direction in which man should proceed. Each was equally sacred in that it was transmitted to Moses at Sinai.

Over the course of approximately five centuries, the Oral Tradition as expounded by the Rabbis developed into an enormous body of law. The need to systematize it was recognized some time prior to the third century of the Common Era. Serving as editor, and utilizing earlier embryonic attempts at systematization, in about 210 C.E. Rabbi Judah HaNasi compiled the Six Orders of The Mishnah. This work, vast in itself, represents the authoritative expression of the Oral Tradition. By means of the practice of its teachings, man is enabled to fulfill completely the will of God as revealed at Sinai. Aboth represents a tractate of the Mishnah. In order to gain a fuller appreciation of its purpose, we shall briefly consider the following: a) its place in the Six Orders of The Mishnah; b) its significance according to Maimonides.

a) Mishnah Aboth appears as the next to the last tractate of Seder Nezikin, the Fourth Order of the Mishnah; "Rabbi Judah (bar Illai) said: He who desires to become saintly, let him fulfill the words of Nezikin; Rabba said, the words of Aboth" (Babba Kamma 30a). Since the Mishnah in its entirety is intended to direct man in the path of ethical conduct, the singling out of tractate Aboth is significant; this can be inferred from a statement of Rabbah: Rabbi Judah (bar Illai) taught all the Mishnayoth in Nezikin, whereas we study all six orders (Ta'anith 24a–b). The implication of the words, ". . . whereas we study all six orders," is that Rabbi Judah taught all the Mishnayoth of the first four orders concluding with Seder Nezikin. For whatever his reasons may have been, his school concluded its studies with the Fourth Order. The likelihood is that tractate Aboth was placed at the conclusion of Seder Nezikin to mark the completion of the study and to summarize the intent of the first four orders of the

Mishnah. The effect then, of the phrase ". . . the words of Nezikin" is that he who desires to become saintly, let him fulfill the words, or sayings, found at the conclusion of Seder Nezikin; Rabba referred to these teachings as the words, or sayings, of Aboth. The original five chapters of Aboth are understood as representing a précis of the principles of proper conduct as taught by the Rabbis. It was directed to the student of Torah as the epitomization of the purpose of his work. As a treatise that teaches principles of ethics, Aboth differs from the other tractates of the Mishnah which deal primarily with law. Nevertheless, like the law, the teachings of Aboth are to be practiced as a rule of everyday life; they are to be lived and affirmed in order to fulfill the object of the Torah.

b) In the Introduction to The Commentary to The Mishnah, Maimonides states that tractate Aboth serves a twofold purpose.

1) It demonstrates the validity of the Oral Tradition as having been given to Moses at Sinai, and that it was transmitted to succeeding generations of teachers who are its authoritative interpreters. The chronological listing at the beginning of Aboth of the groups and individuals who received and transmitted the Oral Tradition establishes the authenticity of their teaching as it unfolded from generation to generation. Thus, Rabbinic interpretations of Biblical statements have the effect of having been given to Moses at Sinai.

2) Tractate Aboth serves to record the words of the sages in order that we may learn moral attributes from them. In The Commentary to Mishnah Aboth, Maimo-

nides views their teachings as intending to develop the person after their ideal character type, the saintly man. In commenting upon one of the mishnayoth, he says ". . . moral instruction is given to man to stimulate him and to improve his soul by means of the moral virtues and the intellectual virtues. For this is the purpose of this tractate."

Maimonides' career as a communal leader represents a hue among many brilliant hues which comprise the spectrum of his life's work. His achievements as an expositor and codifier of Jewish law, and as a philosopher, have had vast impact upon the subsequent development of thought in these areas. Understandably, his labors as a communal official, rooted as they were in the specifics of the events related to the Jewish community of Egypt between 1171 and 1204, appear less lustrous than his great, and more readily appreciated, epoch-making achievements in the fields of law and philosophy. However, Maimonides' endeavors as a communal leader best reflect his essential greatness. It was in this area that he exemplified the Rabbinic ideal of the saintly man. The principles of right conduct as taught in Mishnah Aboth were not merely studied; they were practiced and fulfilled in a saintly manner throughout his long, and oftentimes very trying, career as a leader of the community. This role proved to be the vehicle through which he demonstrated the ideal character type envisioned by the sages of the Mishnah.

As a result of a weak organizational structure compounded by a dearth of competent officials, the Egyptian Jewish community of Maimonides' day was beset by serious problems. Having settled in Egypt in 1165 after fleeing the lands of Almohade persecution, Maimonides obtained a position as a court physician in 1171 under the patronage of the Vizir al-Fadil. However, rather than take the opportunity to devote his available time solely to the pursuit of his scholarly endeavors, in 1171 he assumed an official position as a communal leader. As Dayyan, or chief judge, of the court which formerly functioned as the court of the Nagid (i.e., chief, or leader) of Egyptian Jewry, he attempted to mitigate the effects of a decade of non-existent central communal authority.

Maimonides struggled valiantly to rectify the community's shortcomings. The ideals so ably presented in The Commentary to Mishnah Aboth were given substance through the manner in which he met many serious challenges. Given the limitations imposed by factors outside the community, and considering its spiritually and organizationally deteriorated condition, Maimonides' efforts attest to his being the ideal product of Rabbinic teaching, the scholar who personally engages in the affairs of the community and labors to fashion it into an entity capable of best expressing the values of Judaism.

A number of examples of Maimonides' exceptional virtue will serve to illustrate his saintly character. His attitude toward the Karaite community evidences great forbearance. The Karaites of his day made inroads into the Rabbanite community, scoffing at Rabbanism and denying the validity of the Oral Tradition. The seriousness of their threat can be detected in the

fact that various Rabbanite Jews saw no harm in following Karaite practice. Maimonides did not oppose
the Karaites with scorn and rancor; instead, he sought
to establish harmonious relations with them. He believed that through fostering avenues of amicable contact they might ultimately repent their ways and return to the fold of Rabbanism.

Having personally experienced the dangers of life
in the lands of Almohade persecution, where no doubt
many a Jew rescued himself by reciting the Tauhid,
the Moslem confession of faith, Maimonides was acutely
aware of the danger of informers. Moslem law held no
mercy for a convert to Islam who subsequently aposta-
sized. By virtue of his having fled from the countries
under the sway of the Almohades, Maimonides was
vulnerable to the charge of having at one time rescued
himself by means of reciting the Tauhid. Interestingly,
he and his father wrote treatises defending its recital by
a Jew who did so in order to escape death. They considered it mere lip-service and not a violation of one
of the three cardinal precepts, namely, that of idolatry.
In 1171, the new Egyptian regime elevated to the office
of Nagid a man named Zutta, a known calumniator with
a well-established record of falsely accusing people for
the sake of personal gain. Considering his own personal
history, Maimonides had to have inordinate courage to
have been personally instrumental in bringing about the
deposal of Zutta in 1175. For the sake of the truth, the
preservation of life, and the deliverance of the community from the power of Zutta, he exposed himself
to the possible vengeance of this informer. Indeed, in

1175 he wrote to Yefeth ben Eliyah, ". . . informers have risen up against me to slay me."

In addition to guiding the community of Yemen in spiritual-religious matters, through his close association with the Egyptian government Maimonides was able to assist Yemenite Jewry in the political domain. Moses Naḥmanides attested to the esteem which the Yemenites had for Maimonides. He noted that they accorded Maimonides the extraordinary homage of inserting his name into the recital of the Kaddish out of gratitude for his aid in having certain encumbering decrees nullified, and for effecting a lightening of their tax burden.

No instance demonstrates more clearly the extent of Maimonides' patience and humility than the course he chose to follow when he was deliberately provoked and publicly disparaged by Samuel ben Ali, the Gaon of The Pumbeditha Academy at Baghdad. Monetary rewards served as the underlying motive for a long-protracted dispute between Samuel ben Ali and Samuel of Mosul, the Exilarch at Baghdad, and the latter's predecessor, Daniel ben Ḥisda. At this period, about 1187, owing to the Mishneh Torah which had been published in 1180, Maimonides had achieved great fame as a Halachic authority. In order to counter effectively the Gaon's interpretation of his right to issue Ordination, Samuel of Mosul adduced one of Maimonides' Halachic rulings. Unable to refute this particular ruling, the Gaon and his Ab Beth-Din, Zechariah ben Berachel, embarked upon a campaign of vilification of Maimonides in the hope of diminishing his prestige. They denounced Maimonides as being vain and of having authored the

Mishneh Torah to gain fame. They called attention to various errors, both real and imagined, to deprecate his position as a Halachic authority. Upon receiving a letter from the community of Yemen where certain parties had misunderstood the meaning of Maimonides' teachings with regard to The World To Come and The Messianic Era, the Gaon, whose assistance was sought to clarify these points, took the opportunity to further confuse them. By doing so he implied that Maimonides' teachings lead to heretical misinterpretations of doctrines of faith.

Maimonides maintained a position of aloofness from this sordid controversy. He would not be provoked. He answered his disciple Joseph ibn Aknin's urgent plea to take pen and defend himself by saying, "I will not defend myself. My personal honor as well as my personal ethics decree that I shut my eyes to fools." When Ibn Aknin had apparently taken up the defense of his master in an outspoken manner, Maimonides attempted to subdue his disciple's anger by offering his personal ethics as a guide: "Know, that I strive to act with humility in all matters, even if by so doing it will cause me great harm in the sight of men." Significantly, the longest sections of The Commentary to Mishnah Aboth are devoted to the denunciation of the vices of slander and pride, the praise of humility, and the refutation of those who justify the taking of compensation for their knowledge of Torah.

Although the teachings of the sages as recorded in Mishnah Aboth are intended to inspire man to perfect himself by means of "the moral virtues," the Mishnah does not develop a systematic approach with regard to their acquisition and practice which culminates in a specific goal. In the "Eight Chapters" which serve as an introduction to The Commentary to Mishnah Aboth, Maimonides outlined a system that was influenced by the teachings of Aristotle. Although my notes cover all Maimonides' references to the Eight Chapters, the reader would do well to consult it.

In The Commentary to Mishnah Aboth, Maimonides applied to the teachings of the sages the system that he outlined in the Eight Chapters. In brief, the system may be stated as follows: The wise man's actions are moderate. They are termed "virtues" because they represent the mean between the opposite extremes of excess and deficiency. A deed practiced in either extreme is considered a vice. The saintly man, however, does not practice the precise mean. As a precautionary measure calculated to counterbalance a possible tendency toward an extreme, the saintly man inclines his action somewhat toward its opposite extreme. In only one instance does Maimonides counsel the practice of an extreme. The consequences of the vice of pride are exceedingly harmful, and to mitigate its powerful attraction, Maimonides offers as its sole effective countermeasure the practice of its opposite extreme, namely, humbleness of spirit.

The previously stated examples of Maimonides' personal virtue, to the exclusion of other illustrations which could be offered, lead me to believe that, in his everyday life he endeavored to apply the principles of ethical conduct as taught by the sages in Mishnah Aboth as they were systematically developed by him in The Commentary. The ultimate goal of his systematic approach was the state of prophecy. Saintliness, representing the perfection of the moral virtues, is but a necessary attainment in order to achieve prophecy. The man of God, that is, the prophet, is one who perfects the intellectual virtues as well as the moral virtues. Maimonides believed that the power of the intellect is limited, and that prophecy represents the highest type of perception; through it one could apprehend what was beyond the scope of the intellect. Although he did not explicitly state this as his objective, there can be little doubt that Maimonides aspired to achieve what he believed to be the ultimate form of human perfection, the man of God.

———

A German edition, published by M. Rawicz in 1910, is the only other translation in a European language of The Commentary to Mishnah Aboth. It is hoped that my translation of Samuel ibn Tibbon's Hebrew translation of the Arabic as found in the Wilna edition of the Babylonian Talmud, will afford the English reader a basic appreciation of Mishnah Aboth as understood by Moses Maimonides, post-Talmudic Judaism's greatest spokesman.

With regard to the format of the text, the Roman numerals refer to the enumeration of the Mishnayoth and to their corresponding Commentary. The Mishnah is distinguished from The Commentary by the use of italic type. When the Mishnah is quoted in The Commentary the italics are retained. Quotations from Rab-

binic literature are preceded by a colon, Biblical quotations are denoted by quotation marks. The brackets
indicate my interpolations of both the Mishnah and The
Commentary. Where Hebrew or Aramaic words are
transliterated, they are rendered according to the Ash-
kenazic pronunciation.

CHAPTER

I

*I Moses received the Torah at Sinai and trans-
mitted it to Joshua, and Joshua to the Elders, and
the Elders to the Prophets, and the Prophets transmitted it to the Men of The Great Assembly. They
said three things: Be patient in judgment, raise up
many disciples, and make a fence around the Torah.*

I   In our introduction to this treatise we have elucidated
how the form of the tradition evolved.[1] The only intention here is to explain aught but the words of the
saintly men and the moralists in order to stimulate the acquisition of some of the attributes from them—those

whose benefit is great. Here we shall prolong in cautioning against some of the vices, for their detriment is great.
As for the rest, I shall only define words and some of the
subjects, for except for a few of them, their meanings
are clear.

Be patient in judgment. They should delay issuing
judgment and not decide it hastily so that they may comprehend it. For it is possible that the factors which were
not apparent at the beginning of the consideration will
be revealed to them.

And make a fence around the Torah. He intends to
say the decrees and ordinances which will remove man
from transgressions. As the One to be blessed said,[2]
". . . and you shall keep My charge . . . ," and
through its interpretation it was said: [3] Set a safeguard
about My charge.

> II   *Simeon the Righteous was of the survivors of
> The Great Assembly. He used to say: By three
> things is the world sustained—by the Torah, the
> Temple Service, and deeds of lovingkindness.*

II   He said that by means of wisdom, represented by the
Torah, and by means of the moral virtues, represented
by deeds of lovingkindness, and by means of observing
the precepts of the Torah, represented by the offerings,
shall the perpetual improvement of the world and the
order of its existence be in the perfect path.

> III   *Antigonus of Socho received the tradition
> from Simeon the Righteous. He used to say: Be not*

like servants who serve the master upon the condi-
tion of receiving a gift, but be like servants who
serve the master not upon the condition of receiv-
ing a gift. And let the fear of Heaven be upon you.

III   The benevolence that a man will bestow upon
one to whom he does not owe a favor would be termed
a gift. Indeed, he would do this by way of kindness and
graciousness, as in the instance where a man will say to
his servant, or to his minor son, or to his wife, "Do such
and such for me and I shall give you a dinar or two"—
this constitutes the difference between a gift and a wage,
for a wage is what is given as a matter of legal obligation.

This saintly man said [to his disciples]: You should
not serve the Lord, may He be blessed, upon the condition that He be beneficent to you and bestow kindness
upon you, and thus expect a reward and serve Him for
its sake. Rather, serve Him as servants who do not expect a beneficence nor an act of kindness. By means of
this he intended that they should serve out of love—as
we stated in the tenth chapter of Sanhedrin.[4] Nevertheless, he did not exempt them from [the obligation to
serve Him out of] fear, and he said, that although you
serve Him out of love do not utterly forsake fear, [there-
fore his statement,] *And let the fear of Heaven be upon*
you. For the precept concerning fear was mentioned in
the Torah, as it was said,[5] "Fear the Lord your
God . . . ," and the sages said: [6] Serve out of love, serve
out of fear; and they said, one who serves out of love
will not forget a thing of what he was commanded to
do, and one who serves out of fear will not do a

thing against which he was cautioned. For fear has an important function in the negative precepts, certainly in the precepts whose rationale rests on revelation alone.[7]

This sage had two disciples, one named Zadok and the other named Boethus. When they heard him deliver this statement, they departed from him. The one said to his colleague, "Behold, the master expressly stated that man has neither reward nor punishment, and there is no expectation at all." [8] [They said this] because they did not understand his intention. The one lent support to his colleague and they departed from the community and forsook the Torah.[9]

A sect banded around the one, and another sect around his colleague. The sages termed them "Saducees and Boethusians." Since they were unable to consolidate the masses according to what they perceived of the faith —for this evil belief divided the consolidated, it would certainly not consolidate the divided—they feigned belief in the matter [of the written Torah] because they could not falsify it before the multitude. For had they brought it forth from their mouths, meaning to say, [their disbelief in] the words of the Torah, they would have killed them. Therefore, each said to his party that he believes in the Torah but disputes the tradition since it is not authentic. [They said] this in order to exempt themselves from the precepts of the tradition and the decrees and ordinances inasmuch as they could not thrust aside everything, the written [Torah] and the tradition. Moreover, the path for interpretation was broadened for them. Since the interpretation became a matter of their choice, each, ac-

cording to his intention, could be lenient in what he
might wish or be stringent in what he might wish. [This
was possible] because he did not believe at all in the
fundamental principle. They, however, sought to deceive in matters which were accepted by only some
people.[10]

From the time that these evil sects went forth, they
have been termed "Karaites" in these lands—meaning to
say, Egypt. However, their appellation according to the
sages is "Saducees and Boethusians." They are the ones
who began to contest the tradition and to interpret
all the passages [of the Torah] according to what appeared to them without at all hearkening to a sage;[11]
the reverse of what the One to be blessed stated,[12] ". . .
according to the Torah which they shall instruct you
and according to the judgment which they shall tell
you, you shall do, you shall not turn aside either to the
right or to the left from the sentence which they shall
declare to you."

*IV Jose ben Joezer of Zeredah and Jose ben
Johanan of Jerusalem received the tradition from
them. Jose ben Joezer of Zeredah said: Let your
house be a meeting place for sages, sit amidst the
dust of their feet and drink their words with thirst.*

IV *A meeting place*, [that is,] a house of assembly;
meaning to say that you should make your home always
ready to assemble sages, [just as] in Synagogues and in
houses of study—so that when a man says to his colleague,

"Where shall I come together with you, where shall I meet with you?," he will say to him, "In so and so's home." [13]

> *V   Jose ben Johanan of Jerusalem said: Let your house be opened wide, let the poor be members of your household, and converse not much with a woman. This is said with reference to one's own wife, how much more in the case of his friend's wife. Therefore our sages said: Whenever a man converses much with a woman he causes evil to himself, he desists from the study of Torah, and his end is that he inherits Gehinnom.*

V   *Opened* [means] that you have a gate opened toward the road frequented by travellers, so that any wayfarer who may be in need of anything, or be hungry, or thirsty, may immediately enter the house.[14]

Let the poor be members of your household. He says, the poor and the needy should be your servants and it is more appropriate than purchasing slaves. Thus the sages denounced purchasing slaves and praised him whose servants and household members were the poor.[15]

This is said with reference to one's own wife. It is known that most conversation with women relates to matters of sex. Therefore, he said that indulging in much conversation with them is forbidden, for it *causes evil to himself;* meaning to say that he will acquire moral baseness for his soul, namely, "excessive passion." [16] *He desists from the study of Torah;* it is obvious, for he expends time in other affairs. *And his end is that he inherits Gehinnom,* because this conversation will bring rebelliousness upon him and he will necessitate the punishment for it.[17]

> VI *Joshua ben Peraḥiah and Nittai the Arbelite received the tradition from them. Joshua ben Peraḥiah said: Fashion a teacher for yourself, acquire a friend for yourself, and judge every man in the scale of merit.*

VI *Fashion a teacher for yourself.* Meaning to say, even if he were not suited to be a teacher to you, nevertheless, make him into a teacher for yourself so that you conceive of him that he is teaching, because of this you shall succeed in the study of wisdom. For what a man learns on his own is not on a par with what he learns from someone else, for what he learns on his own is beneficial, however, what he learns from someone else will endure with him longer and it is clearer. [This will obtain] even if he were his equal in wisdom or beneath him; thus they explained through the interpretation of this counsel.[18]

He said, *acquire a friend for yourself.* He mentioned it in the terminology for "acquisition," and he did not say "fashion a friend for yourself" or "befriend others." The intention by means of this is that it is necessary for a man to acquire a friend for himself in order that his deeds and all his interests will be improved through him, as they said: [19] Either fellowship or death. If he would not find him, he should persevere in it with all his heart, even if it would be necessary that he draw him to his friendship until he will become a friend. Let him not turn aside from always adhering to his will so that his friendship may become firm, as the moralists said: When you befriend, do not befriend on your standards; rather, befriend on the standard of your friend. When each of the two friends concentrates on this counsel, the purpose of each of the two will be to promote his friend's will. Thus, the purpose of both jointly will undoubtedly be a single matter. How excellent Aristotle's statement, "The friend is one [with yourself]." [20]

There are three types of friends: the friend of usefulness, the friend of pleasure, the friend of virtue.

Concerning the friend of usefulness—[his friendship is] as the friendship of partners, or as the friendship of a king and his army. The friend of pleasure, however, is of two types: the friend of enjoyment and the friend of trust. Concerning the friend of enjoyment—[his friendship is] as the friendship of males for females, and the like. The friend of trust, however, obtains where a man would have a friend in whom his soul would trust. He would not be guardful of him either in deed or in speech, and he would make known all his interests to him— the good as well as the unseemly, without being apprehensive of him that through all this he would incur disgrace either before him or before someone else. For when a man attains this measure of trust in a person, he shall find great pleasure in his words and in his great fondness.

The friend of virtue obtains where the desire of both, and their purpose, will be related to a single matter, namely, the good, wherein each will wish to assist his friend in attaining that good for both jointly. This is the friend that he counselled to acquire, and it is as the friendship of the master for the disciple and of the disciple for the master.[21]

And judge every man in the scale of merit. Its meaning is [as follows]: Were there a man concerning whom you would not know whether he was righteous or wicked, and you were to observe him perform a deed or utter a word, that if you were to interpret it in one way it would be good, and if you were to interpret it in another way it would be evil, accept him according to the good and do not consider him evil. However, if the man were known to be a righteous man, renowned for good acts, and an act of his was observed all of whose qualities denote that it is an evil act, and no man is able to construe it as good except with great difficulty, and it is a far-fetched possibility, it is proper that you accept it as good, since there is some possibility of its being good, and you are not permitted to suspect him. Concerning this they said: [22] All who suspect the upright will be smitten with bodily afflictions.

Thus, were there a wicked man, and were his deeds widely known, and subsequently we observed him perform a deed all of whose indications denote that it is good, and yet it contains a slight possibility of being evil, it is proper to be guardful of him and not believe that it is good since it contains the possibility of being evil. Concerning this it is said,[23] "Though he makes his voice to be pleasant, do not believe him. . . ."

Were there an unknown man, and the deed did not

incline to one of the two extremes, the way of saintliness requires that you judge in the scale of merit, [that is, by placing it toward an extreme,] whichever extreme of the two extremes it may be.[24]

> *VII   Nittai the Arbelite said: Remove from an evil neighbor, do not befriend the wicked, and do not despair of retribution.*

VII   Do not befriend the wicked through any type of the types of friendship or fellowship in order that you not learn from his deeds. In the introductory chapters we have explained that a man will learn vices in the company of the wicked.[25]

He said, when you sin, or you were to observe a sinner, do not trust and say that the Lord, may He be blessed, will punish him only in The World To Come; rather, do not despair of being speedily avenged by Him for that sin.

> *VIII   Judah ben Tabbai and Simeon ben Shetaḥ received the tradition from them. Judah ben Tabbai said: Do not make yourself as they that prepare the judges. When the litigants are before you, let them be in your sight as wrongdoers, and when they have departed from before you, let them be in your sight as innocent in that they have accepted the judgment.*

VIII   *They that prepare the judges.* They are men who study pleas and laws so that they become experts for people in their litigations. They compose questions and answers [in this manner]: "When the judge says thus, you answer so, and when the [other] litigant argues so, let your reply be thus." It is as if they set in order the judge and the litigants before them. Therefore he termed them *they that prepare the judges*, because it is as if they prepared the judges before them.

He cautioned them (i.e., his disciples) against emulating them, meaning to say, to teach one of the litigants an argument which may avail him by saying to him, "Say thus," or "Deceive in such and such a way." [A judge may not do this] even if concerning him he knew that he is the aggrieved, and that the other party, according to what he considers the truth to be, is alleging a falsehood against him, nevertheless, he is not permitted to teach him an argument which may save him or avail him at all.

IX   Simeon ben Shetaḥ said: Examine the witnesses thoroughly, and be cautious in your words, lest through them they may learn to falsify.

X   Shemaiah and Abtalyon received the tradition from them. Shemaiah said: Love work and despise mastery, and do not make yourself known to the government.

X   *Government.* This refers to the ruling authority. These three rules contain improvement of faith and of mundane affairs. [*Love work,*] for in the absence of work he will be placed in straitened circumstances and he will rob and commit lewdness.[26] [*Despise mastery* means that] in seeking office and mastery he will ex-

perience worldly trials and tribulations. Since people
will be jealous of him and dispute him, he will impair his
faith, as they said: [27] When a man is appointed leader
of a community below, he becomes wicked toward
Heaven.

Thus, knowing the ruler in former times and being
near to him made it very improbable to be delivered
from it (i.e., moral corruption) in this world. It impairs
his faith inasmuch as he would not be concerned with
anything save that which will draw him near to him.
You are aware of the incident of Doeg—even though
the ruler to whom he was near was the anointed of the
Lord, a prophet, and the elect of the Lord, may He be
blessed.[28]

> *XI Abtalyon said: Sages, be cautious of your
> words, lest you incur the penalty of exile, and you
> will be exiled to a place of evil waters, and the dis-
> ciples that come after you will drink and die, thus
> the name of Heaven will be profaned.*

XI *Evil waters* is a figurative expression for heresy. He
said, be vigilant of your words in the midst of the multitude, lest there be among your words an area which would
bear another interpretation. For if there were skeptics
there, they would interpret them in accordance with
their belief. The disciples, having heard them from them,
would turn to heresy and would think that this was
your belief, and through this there would be profanation
of the Name, as happened to Antigonus with Zadok and
Boethus.[29]

XII   Hillel and Shammai received the tradition from them. Hillel said: Be of the disciples of Aaron, loving peace and pursuing peace, loving mankind and drawing them near to the Torah.

XII   *Of the disciples of Aaron.* They said: [30] When Aaron, peace be upon him, would sense that a man was inwardly evil, or when they would tell him that he was inwardly evil and that he was guilty of transgression, he would initiate a peaceful greeting to him, endear himself to him, and converse at length with him. That person would then be embarrassed of himself and say, "Woe to me, had Aaron known what is concealed in my heart and the wickedness of my deeds, he would not have permitted himself to look upon me—much less would he have spoken with me. Yet, in his opinion I am considered as an upright man. Therefore, I will verify his words and thought and I shall turn back to the right path," and he would become one of his disciples who learns from him. When He portrayed him with this honorable attribute, the Lord, may He be blessed, said,[31] ". . . he walked with Me in peace and uprightness and turned many away from iniquity." It was to this quality for which he was renowned that Hillel referred.

XIII   He used to say: A name made great is a name destroyed; he who does not increase will be consumed; he who does not learn is worthy of being executed; and he who makes use of the crown will perish.

XIII   He also said, when a man's name is adhered to greatness, be apprised of its cessation. He also used to say, he who does not increase in study, the Lord, may He be blessed, will put him to death. However, he who has not studied at all is worthy of being executed.[32] *And he who makes use of the crown will perish;* meaning to say, he who earns a livelihood by means of the Torah and derives gain from it. This was his intention through this statement as will be made clear in this tractate.[33] With regard to this it was said by way of an acronym [for the word "TaGA—the crown"]: Talmid (ihn)—[from] a disciple (yes), Gavra Aḥrina (lo)—[from] another man (no). Meaning to say that a scholar is not permitted to accept service from any man except from his disciples.[34]

> *XIV   He used to say: If I am not for myself, who is for me? And when I am for myself, what am I? And if not now, when?*

XIV   [With reference to *If I am not for myself, who is for me?*] He said, if I myself will not be the one who bestirs my soul to virtue, who will bestir it? For it has no external stimulus—as we explained in the Eighth Chapter.[35] [*And when I am for myself, what am I?* is understood to mean]—since it is within my authority to incline my soul to whichever side I desire, which deed of the good deeds have I performed? As if he were derogating himself by saying, "What am I?" As if to say, what has resulted from me, seeing that I am not perfect even though I have performed this matter. Subsequently, he retraced and said [referring to *And if not now, when?*]: If I will not acquire virtues now, in the period of youth, when shall I acquire them—in the period of old age?—no, for it is difficult to turn aside from dispositions at that time because traits and attributes have become firm and permanent, whether virtues or vices. And the sage said,[36] "Train a child in the path he should follow; even when he is old he will not turn aside from it."

> *XV   Shammai said: Set a fixed time for your study of Torah, say little and do much, and greet all men with a pleasant countenance.*

XV   He said, make the study of Torah the root and fundamental point and [let] all the rest of your affairs follow it. If the occasion [to engage in other interests] presents itself, it presents itself, and if the occasion does not present itself, it does not present itself, and there is no harm in its being withheld.[37]

They said: [38] The righteous say little and do much, as Abraham our father, who promised a piece of bread and brought curd, milk, a calf, and three measures of fine meal.[39] The wicked, however, say much yet do not do even a little, as Ephron, who gave everything with his words, yet in practice he did not leave off even a perutah from the price.[40] *With a pleasant countenance* means that one should deal with mankind in gentleness and with pleasant and acceptable words.

XVI   Rabban Gamliel said: Fashion a teacher for yourself, withdraw from doubt, and do not often tithe by estimation.

XVI   This which he counselled here, "to fashion a teacher," does not refer to the subject of "study," but to rendering decision.[41] Establish a preceptor for yourself so that you may rely upon him in [matters pertaining to] the forbidden and the permitted and you will withdraw from doubt. As they said in the Palestinian Talmud: [42] Go, bring me an elder from the marketplace that I may rely upon him, then I will permit you. Thus he counselled that one should flee from extracting tithes by estimation, because it is of the doubtful matters.[43]

XVII   Simeon, his son, said: All my days I have grown up among the sages, and I have found nothing better for a person than silence. The expounding is not the fundamental point, but the practice. And all who multiply words occasion sin.

The sage has said,[44] "In the multitude of words there lacks not trespass. . . ." The reason for this is that the multitude of words [contain words that] are additional, superfluous, and sinful, as I shall presently explain. For when a man multiplies words he will assuredly trespass, since it is impossible that there would not be among his words a word that is not proper to utter. Of the signs of wise men is a lessening of words, and of the signs of fools is a multitude of words, as it is said,[45]

". . . and a fool's voice through a multitude of words."
The sages have said that a lessening of words is evidence of the high station of the parents and that a
man is of pure lineage. They said: [46] In Babylon, silence
is the mark of pure lineage.

It is stated in Sefer HaMiddoth that one of the
sages was observed to be excessively silent in that he
would never speak a word that is not proper to utter,
and that he would speak only very sparingly.[47] It was
said to him, "What is the reason for your excessive
silence?" He said, "I examined all words and I found
them classified into four categories."

The first category: All of it is harm and without
benefit, such as people's cursing, speaking obscenely,
and matters of the like. Words pertaining to them are
utter folly.

The second category: There is harm in it from one
aspect and benefit from the other aspect, such as praising a man in order to derive benefit through it. In that
praise there will be that which will provoke his enemy,
and it will harm the one whom he praised. As a consequence of this reason, it is necessary to forsake words
pertaining to this. [Meaning,] one should also not speak
pertaining to this category.

The third category: Words that have neither benefit
nor harm in them, such as most of the words of the
multitude, [viz.,] how was a certain wall constructed,
how was a certain palace built, and such as describing
the grandeur of a certain building, the abundance of the
produce of a certain province, and matters like these.
They are the words that are superfluous. He said, words

pertaining to this are also superfluous; there is no benefit in them.

The fourth category: Words that all are of benefit,
such as words pertaining to the sciences and the virtues, and a man's speaking concerning what specifically
applies to him, [that is,] of the matters that upon them
his life is dependent and through them his existence will
continue—pertaining to this it is necessary to speak.

He said: Whenever I hear words, I examine them.
If I would find them to pertain to this the fourth category, I will speak of them, and if they were of the
remaining categories, I will keep silent on them. The
moralists said: Examine this man and his wisdom; he
lacks three-fourths of the [categories of] words. This
is the wisdom that should be learned.

I, however, say that according to the requirement
of the Torah, speech should be classified into five categories: 1) Prescribed, 2) Cautioned Against [or Pro-
hibited], 3) Rejected, 4) Desired, 5) Permitted.

The first category is the prescribed, namely, studying
the Torah, teaching it, and studying its Rabbinic learning. This is an obligatory positive precept, as it is said,[48]
". . . and speak of them . . . ," and it is equivalent to
all the precepts. What was stated as admonition with
regard to study is so extensive that this treatise cannot contain part of it.[49]

The second category is the prohibited and cautioned-
against speech, such as bearing false witness, speaking
falsehood, tale-bearing, and cursing. The teachings of
the Torah offer guidance regarding this category;[50]
similarly, obscene speech and slander.

The third category is the rejected speech which has

no benefit in it to man for his soul—purporting neither to transgression nor to rebelliousness, such as most of the discussions of the multitude regarding what has happened and what was, what are the customs of a certain king in his palace, how was so and so's death caused, or how did a certain person become rich. The sages term these [discussions] "idle talk." Saintly men personally persevered to forsake this category of speech. It was said of Rav, the disciple of Rabbi Ḥiyya, that in all his days he never indulged in idle talk.[51] Also pertaining to this category—where a man will denounce virtue or laud vice, be they moral or intellectual.

The fourth category is the desired, namely, speech that is in praise of the intellectual virtues or the moral virtues and simultaneously in denunciation of either of the two types of vices. [As an example,] to bestir the soul to virtues through prose and poetry and to preclude it from vices through those means themselves. Thus, to praise worthy men and to extol their virtues in order that their customs will appear good in the sight of men that they may walk in their ways; and to denounce evil men for their vices in order that their deeds and memory will be condemned in the sight of men that they may remove from them and will not conduct themselves according to their customs. This category, meaning to say, learning the noble attributes and removing from the base attributes, would be termed "derech eretz—proper conduct."

The fifth category is the permitted, namely, speech concerning what specifically applies to man—one's business interest, livelihood, food, drink, clothing, and the rest of what one requires. This is permitted, it is neither desired nor rejected. However, if he wishes, he may speak what he might wish concerning it; and if he wishes, he need not speak. Pertaining to this category, a man is praised when he lessens words in it. Moralists cautioned against multiplying words in it. However, the prohibited and the rejected require neither an admonition nor an exhortation, for it is proper to keep absolutely silent on it.

Concerning the prescribed and the desired—were a man able to speak of it all his days, it would be excellent. However, one needs to be cautious of two things. The first of them—that his deeds be consistent with his words, as they said: [52] Pleasant are the words that emanate from the mouth of one who practices them; and it was to this subject that he referred when he said, *The expounding is not the fundamental point, but the practice.* The sages say to the righteous that he should teach the virtues, as they said: [53] Expound, because it becomes you to expound; and the prophet said,[54] "Rejoice in the Lord, you who are righteous; praise is comely for the upright. . . ." The other matter is brevity; one should strive to multiply the subjects with few words, and that the reverse should not be the case—and it is as they said: [55] One should always instruct his students by way of brevity.

Know, that poetical compositions, in whichever language they may be, should be examined with regard to their themes [in order to determine] whether they follow a manner of speech which we classified. Indeed, I explained this even though this is clear, inasmuch as I have seen elders and saintly men of our co-religionists

when they were at a wine banquet, such as a wedding
or some other occasion, and were a man to wish to recite
an Arabic poem, even if the theme of that poem were
the praise of courage or generosity, and it is of the category of the Desired, or the praises of wine, they would
protest this with every manner of protest, for in their
opinion it is not permitted to listen to it. However,
were the bard to recite any manner of Hebrew poem,
they would not protest it, and it would not be evil
in their sight despite there being in those words [themes
that pertain to] the Cautioned Against or the Rejected.
This is utter folly; since speech shall be neither forbidden, nor permitted, nor desired, nor rejected, nor prescribed in its utterance from the standpoint of the language utilized, but from the standpoint of its subject.
For if the theme of that poem were virtue, it would be
required to recite it in whichever language it may be.
If, however, the purpose of that poem were vice, in
whichever language it may be, it is prohibited to recite
it.

I also have an addendum pertaining to this. For were
there two poems, both having the same theme—arousing
the power of lust, praising it, and causing the soul to
rejoice in it—it is vice, and it is of the category of rejected speech because it stimulates and bestirs a base attribute, as was made clear from our words in the Fourth
Chapter.[56] However, were one of the two poems Hebrew, and the other Arabic or some other non-Hebrew
language, listening to the Hebrew and articulating it
would be more objectionable according to the Torah
due to the exaltedness of the language, for it should only

be utilized for noble purposes—certainly [its use would be prohibited] if it were combined with it by inserting in it a verse from the Torah or from the Song of Songs associated with that theme. For then it departs from the category of the Rejected to the category of the Prohibited and the Cautioned Against, for the Torah prohibited making the words of prophecy into forms of song dealing with vices and unseemly matters.[57]

Since we mentioned slander in the category of prohibited speech, I consider it necessary to explain it and to note concerning it part of what was mentioned, for man is in great blindness with regard to it, and it is the major sin that is always present in man—certainly on the basis of what the sages said: [58] Man is not delivered from the daily involvement in the dust of slander, would that he be delivered from slander itself.

Slander means recounting a man's evil qualities and his blemishes, and to disparage any Israelite with any manner of contumely that it may be, even though the disparaged party were deficient as was mentioned [by the slanderer]. For slander is not a matter where one will lie about a man and attribute to him what he did not do, for this would be termed "spreading evil repute regarding one's fellow." Rather, slander obtains where one will denounce a man even for his deeds which he in truth committed, for one who relates it sins, and one who listens to it sins. They said: [59] Slander slays three parties: one who relates it, one who listens to it, and one of whom it is spoken. And they said: [60] One who receives it [sins] more than one who relates it.

"Dust of slander" means inexplicit mention of a man's blemishes. Pertaining to this subject, Solomon said that at times one who inexplicitly mentions a man's blemishes will pretend that he has no knowledge of what was understood from his words, [e.g.,] that he did not intend this, but he intended another subject, [as he said,] [61] "As a madman who casts firebrands, arrows, and death; so is the man who deceives his neighbor and says, 'Am I not in sport?'" It happened that a certain preparatory student praised the calligraphy of a scribe which was shown to him in the presence of a large assemblage. The master denounced the deed of the praiser of the calligraphy of that scribe and said to him, "Betake yourself from slander." That is to say, that you cause his disparagement when you praise him in the midst of the multitude. For among them are those who love him and among them are those who hate him, and when his enemy hears his praises he will be moved to recall his blemishes and his evil qualities. This is the maximum of removal from slander.[62]

[According to] the language of the Mishnah,[63] the decree upon our forefathers was sealed only because of slander, meaning to say, the subject of the spies, concerning whom it is said,[64] "And they spread an evil report regarding the land. . . ." They, peace be upon them, said: [65] If these who spread an evil report only with regard to trees and stones necessitated the punishment which they deserved, he who will speak in disparagement of his fellow how much more [will he deserve punishment]! [According to] the language of the Tosefta: [66] For three things retribution is exacted from man in this world and he has no share in The World To Come—idolatry, incest, and bloodshed—and slander is equal to all of them. In the Talmud they said: [67] The term "great" was mentioned with regard to [the sin of] idolatry, as it was said,[68] ". . . this people have sinned a great sin. . . ." The term "great" was also mentioned with regard to the sin of incest, as it was said,[69] ". . . how can I do this great wickedness. . . ." The term "great" was also mentioned with regard to the sin of bloodshed, as it was said,[70] ". . . my iniquity is greater than I can bear." However, the term "great things" was mentioned with regard to [the sin of] slander, meaning to say that it is equivalent to the three of them, as it was said,[71] ". . . the tongue speaks great things. . . ." They discussed at great length this sin which arouses; and the ultimate of what was said: [72] Whoever recounts slander has denied the fundamental principle, as it is said, "Who have said, our tongue will we make mighty, our lips are with us, who is lord over us."

In truth, I recounted part of what they related pertaining to this sin even though I have prolonged. [I have done this] in order that man remove from it with all his ability, and that he make it his purpose to keep silent, meaning to say, on this category of speech.

XVIII   Rabban Simeon ben Gamliel said: By three things is the world sustained—by truth, judgment, and peace. As it is said, ". . . execute the judgment of truth and peace in your gates" (Zechariah 8:16).

XVIII *Judgment* refers to governing the state with uprightness. In the Fourth Chapter we have explained that *truth* refers to the intellectual virtues, and *peace* refers to the moral virtues.[73] Were these three to be found, existence would undoubtedly be in the state of perfection that is possible for it [to attain].

2

*1 Rabbi [Judah HaNasi] said: Which is the
straight path that a man should choose for himself? Whichever is an honor to one who practices it and gets him honor from men. And be
heedful of a light precept as of a weighty one, for
you do not know the payment of the recompense
for the precepts. And reckon the loss [incurred
through the non-fulfillment] of a precept against
its recompense, and the recompense [obtained
through the non-commission] of a transgression
against its loss. Reflect upon three things and you
will not come into the power of transgression; know*

what is above you—a seeing eye, a hearing ear, and all your deeds are recorded in a book.

I It is clear that the straight path refers to the good acts, as we explained in the Fourth Chapter, and they are of the virtues that are midway.[1] For through them a man will acquire a worthy disposition for his soul and his manner with people will be good. As it was said, . . . *an honor to one who practices it and gets him honor from men.*

Subsequently, he said that it is necessary to be as heedful of the precept which one will reckon to be light, such as rejoicing on the festival or teaching the sacred language,[2] as with the precept whose weightiness was made clear to you that it is great, such as circumcision, fringes, and the sacrifice of the paschal lamb.[3] He offered as reason for this, *for you do not know the payment of the recompense for the precepts.*

The explanation of this subject is as I shall state, that is, the Torah in its entirety is comprised of positive precepts and negative precepts.[4] Concerning the negative precepts, except for a few of them,[5] Scripture made clear the punishment for each of them. For some it required Execution,[6] for some Extirpation,[7] or Death by An Act of Heaven, or Stripes.[8] From the punishments for the negative precepts, we know, concerning all of them, which of them constitutes a major prohibition and which of them is beneath it. They are [classified in] eight degrees.

The first degree, this being the severest among them, they are the matters which require Stoning. The degree beneath it, those that require Burning. The third, those that require Sword. The fourth, those that require Strangulation. The fifth, those that require Extirpation. The sixth, those that require Death by An Act of Heaven. The seventh, those that require Stripes. The eighth, negative precepts for which one does not receive Stripes.[9] From these degrees we may know the weightiness of the iniquity or its lightness.

Concerning the positive precepts, it was not made clear what the recompense is according to the Lord, may He be blessed, for any of them. All this [was intended] in order that we may not know which precept requires diligent observance and which precept is beneath it. However, it commanded one to practice this matter and that matter and did not make known which of the two bears the greater recompense according to the Lord, may He be blessed, therefore it is necessary to be heedful of all of them. As a consequence of this principle they said: [10] One who is engaged in a precept is exempt from the [obligation to fulfill some other] precept; [this was taught in order that he proceed] without comparing the precept he is engaged in with the other from which he was withheld. Therefore, they also said: [11] We do not pass by the precepts; meaning to say, when the occasion for practicing a precept presents itself to you, do not pass it by and forsake it to practice some other precept.

Subsequently, he said that although the measure of the dearness of one precept as against another precept was not made clear, they have an aspect through which they may be compared. That is, that every positive precept concerning which you will find that one who passes it by shall necessitate a severe punishment, know that in practicing it there is also a great recompense. The illustration of this—circumcision, paschal offering,[12] resting on the seventh [day],[13] and making a parapet,[14] all these are positive precepts. However, the requirement for one who performs work on the Sabbath is Stoning,[15] whereas one who neglects circumcision,[16] or a seasonal offering,[17] requires Extirpation,[18] while one who brings blood upon his house is [guilty of transgressing] a negative precept [which does not require the punishment of Stripes],[19] as it was said,[20] ". . . that you bring not blood upon your house. . . ." From this you may know that the recompense for resting on the Sabbath is greater than the recompense for circumcision, and the recompense for circumcision is greater according to the Lord, may He be blessed, than the recompense for making a parapet.[21] This is the meaning of his statement, *And reckon the loss [incurred through the non-fulfillment] of a precept against its recompense.*[22]

[With reference to reckoning . . . *the recompense [obtained through the non-commission] of a transgression against its loss.*] He also said, the recompense [obtained] when you do not commit a transgression, this, too, was not made clear. However, you may deduce it[s recompense which is received for non-commission] from its punishment [which is necessitated by commission]. For the sin where the punishment for one who commits it is great, the recompense for his forsaking it is as that same measure in magnitude—as was made clear in Kiddushin, when they said:²³ Whoever desists and does not commit a transgression is given a recompense as one who practices a precept—we have explained it there.²⁴

[With reference to . . . *and all your deeds are recorded in a book.*] The language of the Torah [verifies that God is omniscient], since deeds are known before Him, may He be blessed, as Moses, our master, peace be upon him, said,²⁵ ". . . from Your book which You have written. . . ."

> II   *Rabban Gamliel, the son of Rabbi Judah Ha-Nasi, said: Study of Torah along with worldly occupation is seemly, for labor in them both causes sin to be forgotten. All [study of] Torah without work comes to naught and leads to sin. Let all who toil for the community toil with them for the sake of Heaven. For the merit of their fathers sustains them and their righteousness endures forever. And you I consider worthy of great recompense as though you had practiced.*

II   Here, through the term "derech eretz—worldly occupation," he intended to say, being engaged in earning a livelihood. [The meaning of] his statement, . . . *and leads to sin,* is as we explained in another place,²⁶ [as] they said: ²⁷ He ends by robbing from mankind.

When he said, *And you I consider worthy of great recompense as though you had practiced,* it is [to be understood as] the word of the Lord to those who toil with the community. For at times, while they are engaged in the needs of the community they will be precluded from practicing a precept. He said that the Lord, may He be blessed, will consider them worthy of recompense as though they had practiced that precept even though they did not practice it, since they were engaged with the community for the sake of Heaven.

> *III Be cautious with the government for they do not draw a man near except for their own needs. They appear to be as friends at such time as it is to their advantage, but they do not stand by a man at the time of his urgency.*

III We have explained that *the government* refers to the ruling authority in former times.[28] He describes their attributes and cautions against them.

> *IV He used to say: Make His will as your will, in order that He make your will as His will. Nullify your will before His will, in order that He nullify the will of others before your will. Hillel said: Do not separate yourself from the community, and do not be sure of yourself until the day of your death, and judge not your fellow until you have come into his place. Say not a word which cannot be understood that it will be understood in the end. And do not say, "When I have leisure I will study"; perhaps you will have no leisure.*

IV In the Fourth Chapter we have made known that one should not separate from the community except in accordance with their (i.e., its members') corruption, as we explained it there.[29]

He said that although a man may have a worthy disposition in his soul which has become firm, in order to increase the firmness he should not withdraw his hand from repeating the practice of the good. Let him not trust and say, "I have achieved this virtue and it is impossible for it to depart," for it is possible that it may depart, as it was said, *until the day of your death.*

. . . *A word which cannot be understood* means that the literal meanings of the words will be abstruse and vacuous, and when a man carefully reflects upon them he will perceive that the words are intelligible. He cautions against that manner of speech, for he said, let not your words require far-fetched interpretation and inordinate reflection that only then the listener will understand them.

"*When I have leisure. . . ,*" meaning thereby, when I will be at leisure from this endeavor. This is similar to what was previously stated in his colleague Shammai's counsel—*Set a fixed time for your study of Torah.*[30]

> V   *The empty man does not fear sin, the ignorant man cannot be saintly, the diffident man cannot learn, and the impatient man cannot teach, and not all who engage much in commerce become wise. In a situation where there are no men, strive to be a man.*

V   *The empty man* is one who does not have either wisdom or [moral] attributes. *The ignorant man* is one who does not have intellectual virtues but has some moral virtues. *The diffident man,* as understood.[31] *The impatient man* is he who is exacting in all matters and is given to anger.

The meaning of "hishtadel—strive": habituate your soul and draw it to acquire the virtues. Since there are no wise men there who may instruct you, you be the one who instructs yourself. The Targum renders "va-'yeyaveyk ish imo—and a man wrestled with him" as "v'ishtadal gavra imeh—and a man strove with him." [32]

[With reference to . . . *and not all who engage much in commerce become wise.*] They said: [33] [Knowledge of] the Torah will not be found in proud and haughty men nor in those who journey to distant lands. They juxtaposed this with a verse from the standpoint of an allegory; as it was said, "It is not in heaven that you should say [who will ascend. . .], Nor is it beyond the sea. . . ," they said: It is not in the haughty nor is it in those who journey beyond the sea.[34]

> *VI   Moreover, he saw a skull floating on the face of the water. He said: Because you have drowned [others], they drowned you, and in the end they that drowned you will be drowned.*

VI Meaning to say, you were killed because you killed someone else, and that the one who killed you is destined to be killed. The intention by means of this statement is that evil acts will be returned upon the heads of those who do them, as it was said,[35] "His own iniquities will ensnare the wicked . . ."; and it was said,[36] "He dug a pit, hollowed it, [and fell into the ditch he made.]" The sages said: [37] By the standard with which a man measures, with it they measure him. This is a matter that is apparent to the inner eye in every time, in every period, and in every place—that everyone who will do evil and devise forms of wrongdoing and vices, he himself will be injured by those evil deeds themselves which he devised, for he taught the art which will do harm to him and to someone else. Thus, whoever teaches virtue which brings into being any manner of good act, he will attain the benefit of that act, for he taught the matter which will do good to him and to someone else. The words of Scripture pertaining to this are excellent, he said,[38] "The work of a man will He requite unto him, [and according to the way of a man will He cause him to find.]"

VII   He used to say: The more flesh, the more worms; the more possessions, the more worry; the more women, the more witchcraft; the more maidservants, the more lewdness; the more men-servants, the more theft. The more Torah, the more life; the more schooling, the more wisdom; the more counsel, the more sagacity; the more righteousness, the more peace. He who has acquired a good name has acquired it for himself. He who has acquired the words of the Torah has acquired the life of The World To Come.

VIII   Rabban Joḥanan ben Zakkai received the tradition from Hillel and Shammai. He used to say:

If you have learned much Torah do not claim credit for yourself, for it was for this that you were fashioned. Rabban Johanan ben Zakkai had five disciples, and these are they: Rabbi Eliezer ben Hyrcanus, Rabbi Joshua ben Hananiah, Rabbi Jose the Priest, Rabbi Simeon ben Nathanel, and Rabbi Elazar ben Arach. He used to recount their praises: Rabbi Eliezer ben Hyrcanus is a plastered cistern which does not lose a drop; Rabbi Joshua ben Hananiah, praised is she who bore him; Rabbi Jose the Priest is a saintly man; Rabbi Simeon ben Nathanel is a sin-fearing man; and Rabbi Elazar ben Arach is like a full-flowing spring. He used to say: If all the sages of Israel were in one scale of the balance and Rabbi Eliezer ben Hyrcanus in the second scale, he would outweigh them all. Abba Saul said in his name: If all the sages of Israel were in one scale of the balance and even Rabbi Eliezer ben Hyrcanus with them, and Rabbi Elazar ben Arach in the second scale, he would outweigh them all.

VIII Rabbi Eliezer was praised for excellent memory by likening him to a limed cistern which will not lose its waters. Rabbi Joshua was lauded for moral virtues, for through them a man will be praised and honored, and most people will love him; therefore, through him he praises she who bore him. Rabbi Jose was extolled for excellence in moral virtues and in intellectual virtues. Rabbi Simeon was praised for [being] sin-fearing, that is, [his] zealousness and diligence in mat-

ters of engaging in the good and his vigilance of evil.
Rabbi Elazar ben Arach was lauded for skillfulness in
comprehension, since every profound subject was simple
to him and his sagacity added to the subject.

> *IX   He said to them: Go and see which is the*
> *straight path to which a man should cleave. Rabbi*
> *Eliezer said, a good eye. Rabbi Joshua said, a good*
> *colleague. Rabbi Jose said, a good neighbor. Rabbi*
> *Simeon said, one who sees what is to be. Rabbi*
> *Elazar said, a good heart. He said to them: I ap-*
> *prove the words of Rabbi Elazar ben Arach, for*
> *your words are included in his words. He said to*
> *them: Go and see which is the evil path that a man*
> *should remove from. Rabbi Eliezer said, an evil eye.*
> *Rabbi Joshua said, an evil colleague. Rabbi Jose*
> *said, an evil neighbor. Rabbi Simeon said, one who*
> *borrows and does not repay. One who borrows*
> *from man is as one who borrows from the Omni-*
> *present, as it is said, "The wicked borrows and does*
> *not repay, but the righteous is gracious and gives"*
> *(Psalms 37:21). Rabbi Elazar said, an evil heart. He*
> *said to them: I approve the words of Rabbi Elazar*
> *ben Arach, for your words are included in his*
> *words.*

IX   *A good eye* refers to contentedness with that which
a man possesses, and it is of the moral virtues. *An evil
eye* is its opposite, meaning to say—belittling of things
and the lust for gain.

He stated here . . . *one who sees what is to be;*

its meaning is that he will deduce what is destined to be from that which presently exists. This is not [classified] in scientific knowledge until it will be an intellectual virtue; its definition will then be, he will deduce the hidden from the obvious. However, here by means of this [statement] he intends [to refer to] the speculation upon human affairs, [that is,] from one's interests through which his existence continues, he should speculate upon the future of his affairs.[39] Over against this he adduced an example; as it was said, . . . *one who borrows and does not repay*—one will not lend him a thing afterwards, and this constitutes moral baseness. "But the righteous is gracious and gives"—this refers to the Righteous One of the world, that is, the Lord, may He be blessed, as it is said,[40] "He is just and righteous." Thus, "You are just in all that is come upon us . . . ,"[41] meaning: He is gracious to the man who lends to his fellow and is not repaid; the Holy One, blessed be He, repays him the exchange for his service wherein he bestowed kindness to another by lending him so that he had the means sufficient for his need, and when he had the means and did not repay his lender, the Lord, may He be blessed, repaid him.

The meaning of "he approves his words" [is that] he selects and differentiates, as derived from the meaning [of the verse], ". . . the Lord does not approve;"[42] its intention is, He did not select and differentiate. For everything is included in his words wherein he stated *an evil heart.*[43]

In the Second Chapter which we prefaced to The Commentary on this tractate we have explained that all the moral virtues belong only to the Appetitive Faculty of the faculties of the soul, and the moral vices also belong to it.[44] In the Fourth Chapter we explained that acts that are good are the acts that are midway which will ensue from the moral virtues.[45] Thus it is known by philosophers and physicians that the Appetitive [Faculty of the] soul is in the heart, the heart is its chamber and vessel, and it (i.e., the Appetitive Faculty) is related to it (i.e., the heart). Although, according to genuine knowledge, all the powers spread from the heart, and it is their initiator, the appetitive power, however, does not emanate from it to another organ in the same way that the nutritive power emanates—meaning to say, the Growing Faculty, as we described it in the First Chapter, [as an example,] from the heart to the liver.[46]

You are to understand from all that we explained that by *a good heart* he means the good acts, they are the acts that are midway, and they are moral virtues; it includes contentedness, befriending good men, and virtues other than these, as it was said, . . . *for your words are included in his words.* Thus, *an evil heart* refers to moral vices and it also includes all that they cautioned against.

> X   *They [each] said three things. Rabbi Eliezer said: Let your friend's honor be dear to you as your own; be not easy to provoke; and repent one day before your death. Be warmed before the fire of the sages, but be cautious of their glowing coals lest you be burned. For their bite is the bite of a fox, and their sting the sting of a scorpion, and*

*their hiss the hiss of a serpent, and all their words
are like coals of fire.*

X *Be not easy to provoke* [means] do not ready yourself to anger and fury. They have hyperbolized in de-
nouncing anger and fury, and the severest among their
teachings is their statement: [47] Everyone who is given
to anger is as if he worships an idol. They juxtaposed
this with the statement,[48] "Neither let there be a strange
god in you (i.e., anger) nor shall you bow down to a
foreign god (i.e., idolatry)," meaning to say that the
two matters are equal.

And repent one day before your death. One does not
know when one will die—perhaps today, perhaps to-
morrow; thus let all one's days be in repentance.

However, his statement, *Be warmed before the fire
of the sages,* is not of the statements with which he re-
proved. Rather, it is from what he heard from someone
else and he used to relate it, therefore it was not ex-
cluded from his total teaching. The intention through
this counsel is—that he said to you: When you befriend sages and magnanimous men, be neither familiar
with them nor overbearing toward them. Rather, let
their friendship be [of such manner whereby you are
able] to make known to them that you will draw near
at the time that they will draw you near. Do not continue to draw near to them beyond that which they
will draw you near, lest you impair their impression of
you and their love will turn into enmity, and you will
not obtain from them the benefit which you expect. He
compared this with one who warms himself at a fire:

If he were to sit at a proper distance from it, he would derive pleasure in its warmth and will profit through its light. However, if he were to act with negligence toward himself and would continue to draw near to it, he would be burned, and the benefit will become harm to him. This is the meaning of his statement by way of the parable, *Be warmed before the fire of the sages, but be cautious of their glowing coals lest you be burned.*

Subsequently, based on this, he continued to warn and said, do not think that if they were to bite you with their tongue you may return and placate them with words and they will be mollified. In truth, they will not hearken to the voice of the charmer, just as the serpent does not hearken to it, as it was said,[49] "[. . . they are like the deaf asp that shuts her ear.] Which does not hearken to the voice of charmers. . . ." You may know this from the incident of Geḥazi in which he acted with effrontery toward his master Elisha, for he was smitten with a loathsome malady,[50] as was made clear from the words of the sages with regard to the subject of "And there were four leprous men. . . ."[51] Similarly [in the incident of Jesus the Nazarene] with Rabbi Joshua ben Peraḥiah.[52] In each instance the detriment which they incurred was made clear, and others who overstepped the bounds of propriety.

> *XI   Rabbi Joshua said: An evil eye, an evil inclination, and hatred of mankind remove a man from the world.*

XI   He said that lust for money, excessive passion, and evil spiritedness—that is, the malady of melancholia which will bring a man to disdain what his eyes behold and he will loathe it [53]—the company of beasts and solitude in deserts and in forests will be beneficial to him, and an area that is uninhabited will be preferable to him—this [type of withdrawal] on their part is not from the standpoint of "separateness," but [it is to be attributed] to the evilness of their passion and their envy of others; these [traits] will undoubtedly put a man to death, for his body will become sick and he will die before his time. [54]

XII   Rabbi Jose said: Let your friend's property be dear to you as your own; prepare yourself to study Torah, for it is not yours by inheritance; and let all your deeds be for the sake of Heaven.

XII   In the Eighth Chapter we have explained the meaning of predisposition and predilection, [viz.,] that it is necessary for man to prepare himself for [the acquisition of] virtues. [55] In the Fifth Chapter we explained the meaning of his statement, *and let all your deeds be for the sake of Heaven.* [56]

XIII   Rabbi Simeon said: Be heedful in reading the Shema and the Tefillah.[1] And when you pray, do not make your prayer a fixed regimen; rather, [let it be a supplication for] mercy and graciousness before the Omnipresent, as it is said, "For He

1. *The Shema: Deuteronomy 6:4–9, 11:13–21; Numbers 15:37–41. The Tefillah: The Eighteen Benedictions and one additional, Megillah 17b, Berachoth 29a.*

is a gracious and merciful God, long-suffering and
abundant in kindness and repents of the evil"
(Joel 2:13). And do not consider yourself wicked.

XIII   When a man considers himself deficient and base,
a deficient act which he might perform will not be mag-
nified in his sight.

We have explained that the meaning of *fixed regimen*
is that prayer will be burdensome to him, and he will
consider it as if he were commanded to occupy himself
with a certain affair and that he may rest from it.[57]

> *XIV   Rabbi Elazar said: Be watchful to study*
> *Torah; know what to reply to a heretic, and know*
> *before whom you toil. The master of your task*
> *is faithful to pay you the recompense of your*
> *work.*

XIV   The meaning of watchfulness is derived from the
language of the verse,[58] ". . . for I am watchful of My
word. . . ," that is to say, [He is] prompt and diligent.
Or, its meaning may be, habit and constancy, as [in
the verse,] ". . . watching daily at my gates. . . ."[59]

. . . *What to reply to a heretic.* . . . He said, it is
necessary that you learn subjects so that you may give
reply with them to the atheists of idolatrous peoples;
you should dispute them and answer them if they question you.[60] They said: [61] This applies only to a gentile
atheist; however, in the case of a Jewish heretic, [if
you were to dispute him] he would certainly advocate

heretical opinions all the more, meaning to say, he will scoff even more. Consequently, one should not speak to him at all, for there is no remedy for him, nor any cure for him whatsoever, as it is said,[62] "None who go to her will return, nor do they attain the paths of life."

He said that although you may learn the knowledge of the nations to know how to reply to them, be vigilant lest aught of those disciplines enter your heart, and know that He before whom you labor is cognizant of what is concealed in your heart, as it was said, . . . *and know before whom you toil*, meaning to say that he should direct his heart to belief in the Lord, may He be blessed.

> *XV   Rabbi Tarfon said: The day is short, the task is great, and the workers are slothful, yet the recompense is great and the master of the house is urgent.*

XV   This is a parable concerning the brevity of years, the great amount of wisdom [to be acquired] and man's slothfulness in seeking it, despite the great amount of recompense for it, and despite the multitude of the Torah's admonitions and its exhortations to seek wisdom and learning.

> *XVI   He used to say: It is not for you to finish the task, nor are you free to desist from it. If you have learned much Torah you will be given a great recompense. The master of your task is faithful*

*to pay you the recompense of your work. And
know that the payment of the recompense to the
righteous is in the time to come.*

XVI . . . *In the time to come,* meaning to say, in The
World To Come. We have explained the meaning of
The World To Come in the tenth chapter of San-
hedrin in which it was appropriate to mention it.[63]

3

I   *Akabya ben Mahalalel said: Reflect upon three matters and you will not come into the power of transgression. Know whence you came, and where you are going, and before whom you are to give an account and reckoning. Whence you came—from a fetid drop. And where you are going—to the place of dust, worms, and maggots. And before whom you are to give an account and reckoning—before the King of kings, the Holy One, blessed be He.*

I   This reflection brings man into the power of modesty through the rememberance of whence he came. His reflecting upon his future will bring him to spurn mundane matters, and his reflecting upon the greatness of the One who ordains will bring him to be quick to obey His precepts. When he achieves these three matters he will not sin at all.

II   Rabbi Ḥanina the Deputy of the Priests said: Pray for the welfare of the kingdom, for were it not for the fear of it men would swallow each other alive. Rabbi Ḥanina ben Teradion said: Where two sit and no words of the Torah are exchanged between them, this is the company of scorners, as it is said, ". . . nor sits in the company of scorners. . . ."(Psalms 1:1). However, where two sit and words of the Torah are exchanged between them the Divine Presence abides with them, as it is said, "Then they who feared the Lord spoke one to another, the Lord hearkened and heard, and a book of rememberance was written before the Lord for them who feared the Lord and that thought upon His name" (Malachi 3:16). We have proven the case of two, whence do we obtain that even if one sits and engages in the Torah, the Holy One, blessed be He, establishes a recompense for him? As it is said, "Let him sit in solitude and keep still because He has cast it upon him" (Lamentations 3:28).

II   His proof that every place where words of the Torah are not discussed would be termed . . . *the company of scorners* is derived from the conclusion of the verse where it said,[1] "But his delight is in the Torah of the Lord. . . ." It is as if it said that because his delight was in the Torah of the Lord he did not sit in the company of scorners, since it does not contain the Torah of the Lord.

Whence do we obtain that even if one sits. . . . In the first chapter of Berachoth it is stated in this language: [2] Whence do we obtain that one who sits and engages in the Torah that the Divine Presence is with him?—as it is said,[3] ". . . in every place where I cause my name to be mentioned I will come to you and bless you." Since this is so even in the case of one, what need is there to inform us that it is so in the case of two? In the case of two their words are inscribed in the book of rememberances; in the case of one, his words are not inscribed. Since this is so even in the case of two, what need is there to inform us that it is so in the case of three [who are convened as a court of law]? You might say that the act of a court of law refers only to settling disputes, and the Divine Presence will not come [and abide among those convened as a court of law]! We are therefore informed that the act of a court of law is also to be considered as studying Torah [and the Divine Presence will abide among them]. Since this is so even in the case of three, what need is there to inform us that it is so in the case of ten [who comprise a quorum for prayer]? In the case of ten, the Divine Presence arrives prior [to their being fully assembled]. Whereas in the case of three [who constitute a court of law, the Divine Presence abides among them] after they are seated.[4]

The meaning of "v'yidom—and keep still," refers to covert speech, as derived from "kol d'mamah dakah— a still, small voice." [5] Derived from this, the Targum translated "va'yidom aharon—and Aaron kept still," [6] as "u'sh'thayk aharon—and Aaron kept silent." His (i.e., Rabbi Ḥanina ben Teradion's) proof that he [who engages in the Torah in solitude] is as one who fulfilled the entire Torah, is derived from the statement, ". . . *because He has cast it upon him*"; [that is,] it is as if the giving of the entire Torah was for his sake alone.[7]

> *III   Rabbi Simeon said: Three who have eaten at one table and have not discussed words of the Torah over it, it is as if they had eaten of the sacrifices of the dead, as it is said, "For all the tables are full of vomit and filth with no space ("makom")" (Isaiah 28:8). However, three who have eaten at one table and discussed words of the Torah over it, it is as if they had eaten of the table of the Omnipresent ("makom"), as it is said, ". . . and He said to me, this is the table that is before the Lord" (Ezekiel 41:22).*

III   *Sacrifices of the dead* would be termed "offerings for the worship of an idol," just as Scripture termed it, as we explained in the third chapter of Abodah Zarah.[8] Isaiah also termed it "vomit and filth" in order to express contempt for it, just as an idol itself would be termed "idols and detestable things." [9] He (i.e., Rabbi Simeon) preceded this verse with a passage which denotes one who is occupied with food and drink and the forsaking of the Torah and its Rabbinic learning.[10] Consequently, all the tables were as if they had eaten the abhorrent and filthy things upon them, meaning to say, food offered for the worship of idols, and he stated it before this verse—"These too reel through wine and stagger through strong drink. . . . [For all the tables are full of vomit and filth with no space ("makom")]."[11]

IV   Rabbi Ḥanina ben Ḥachinai said: One who awakens at night and walks in solitude on the road and turns his heart to vain things forfeits his soul.[12]

V   Rabbi Neḥunya ben HaKanah said: Whoever takes upon himself the yoke of the Torah, they remove from him the yoke of the kingdom and the yoke of worldly occupation. However, whoever casts off the yoke of the Torah, they place upon him the yoke of the kingdom and the yoke of worldly occupation.

V   *The yoke of the Torah* [means] the constancy of study. *The yoke of the kingdom* [means] the burden of the king and his armies. *The yoke of worldly occupation* [means] the burden of fortune.[13] He said that in recompense for his assuming the yoke of the Torah, the Lord, may He be blessed, will deliver him and relieve him of the burden of fortune. His statement, *casts off the yoke of the Torah*, refers to one who said, "The Torah was not Divinely revealed and I will not bear

it." [14] They said: [15] "Ḥaruth—engraved" upon the tablets [means] "ḥeruth—freedom" upon the tablets;
meaning to say, freedom from the consequences of fortune and from the affairs of kings is granted to one who
accepts and practices what is written upon the tablets.

> *VI   Rabbi Ḥalafta of K'far Ḥanania said: If ten
> men sit together and engage in the Torah, the
> Divine Presence abides among them, as it is said,
> "God stands in the congregation of God . . . ."
> (Psalms 82:1). From whence do we obtain that this
> is so even in the case of five? As it is said, "He has
> founded His group upon the earth" (Amos 9:6).
> From whence do we obtain that this is so even in
> the case of three? As it is said, ". . . in the midst of
> the judges ("elohim") He judges" (Psalms, loc.
> cit.). From whence do we obtain that this is so even
> in the case of two? As it is said, "Then they who
> feared the Lord spoke one to another and the Lord
> hearkened and heard. . . ." (Malachi 3:16). From
> whence do we obtain that this is so even in the case
> of one? As it is said, "In every place where I record
> my name I will come to you and bless you"
> (Exodus 20:24).*

VI   *"In the congregation of God. . . ."* Behold, at the
beginning of Sanhedrin we explained that "congregation" does not apply to less than ten. There too, we explained that a court of law is not less than three, and
they (i.e., the judges) are termed "elohim" with regard to the subject of executing judgment. [16]

The meaning of "agudah—group," refers to what a man clenches ("oged") in one hand, the hand has five fingers with which it clenches, and the containment of five fingers would also be termed "agudah—group." [17]

VII   Rabbi Elazer of Bartotha said: Give Him what is His, for you and what is yours are His. Thus concerning David it is said, ". . . for all things come of You and of Your own hand have we given You" (I Chronicles 29:14). Rabbi Jacob said: One who walks along the road and studies, and interrupts his study and remarks, "How beautiful is this tree, how beautiful is this furrowed field," Scripture reckons him as though he forfeited his soul.

VIII   Rabbi Dostai bar Jannai said in the name of Rabbi Meir: Whoever forgets one word of his study, Scripture reckons him as though he forfeited his soul, as it is said, "Only take heed to yourself, and keep your soul diligently, lest you forget the things which your eyes have seen. . . ." (Deuteronomy 4:9). You might assume that this applies even in the case where his study was too hard for him. Scripture teaches otherwise in saying, ". . . and lest they depart from your heart all the days of your life" (Ibid.). Thus, he does not forfeit his soul unless he purposefully removes them from his heart.

*IX   Rabbi Ḥanina ben Dosa said: Everyone whose
fear of sin precedes his wisdom, his wisdom endures.
Whereas everyone whose wisdom precedes his fear
of sin, his wisdom will not endure. He used to say:
Everyone whose deeds exceed his wisdom, his wisdom endures. Whereas everyone whose wisdom
exceeds his deeds, his wisdom will not endure.*

IX   Behold, this matter is also agreed upon by the philosophers: when the habit of [moral] virtues precedes
wisdom until it will be a firm trait, and afterwards
one were to study wisdom which would stimulate him
toward those good qualities, he would increase in delight
and love of wisdom and in determination to add to it,
since it would bestir him toward what was habituated.[18]
However, when evil traits precede, and afterwards one
were to study, wisdom would preclude him from what
he would desire through habit.[19] Wisdom would be burdensome to him and he would forsake it.

*X   He used to say: Everyone in whom the spirit
of mankind takes pleasure, the spirit of the Omnipresent takes pleasure. Whereas everyone in whom
the spirit of mankind takes no pleasure, the spirit of
the Omnipresent takes no pleasure. Rabbi Dosa ben
Harkinas said: Morning sleep, midday wine, children's talk, and sitting in the meeting-houses of
ignorant men remove a man from the world.*

X   [With reference to *Morning sleep.* . . .] He said,
these matters preclude [the attainment of virtue] and

nullify a man's virtue until he departs from the world and he perishes.[20]

> *XI   Rabbi Elazar of Modi'im said: One who profanes sacred things, one who contemns the appointed festivals, one who puts his fellow to shame in public, one who abrogates the covenant of Abraham our father, and one who interprets the Torah at variance with the Halachah, even though he possesses knowledge of the Torah and good deeds, he has no share in The World To Come.*

XI   *Puts his fellow to shame in public* means he who embarrasses his fellow. *Interprets the Torah . . .* means he who transgresses the precepts of the Torah in public, and it is the ultimate of denial [of the existence of God], as the Lord, may He be blessed, said,[21] "The soul who acts high-handedly . . . [blasphemes the Lord]." The meaning of "m'galleh panim—interprets"—he will interpret and be brazen. This is the terminology regarding denial and it is explained thusly in the Talmud to Peah—they said: [22] *One who interprets the Torah at variance with the Halachah* [means] one who transgresses the teachings of the Torah in public as Jehoiakim, the son of Josiah. *Abrogates the covenant* is to be taken literally.[23] There it stated with reference to all the matters concerning which the sages said that one who does them has no share in The World To Come: [24] How are we to understand this? If he had repented, there is nothing that stands before the repentant.[25] Rather, it refers to when he did not repent and died in chastisement, meaning to say that the weightiness of the sins—they are the ones concerning which they noted *he has no share in The World To Come* —is greater than other sins, for chastisement with death will not atone for them.[26]

XII   Rabbi Ishmael said: Be plain before one in authority, be placid to youth, and greet ("m'kabel") all men with cheerfulness.

XII   "Plainness" is understood.[27] *Placid* means calmness and patience. By means of this counsel he said, when you stand before a man of high station, make yourself plain before him. Render service to him and stand before him as he would wish, and do not assume self-importance toward him.[28] However, when you are with one of dark hair, meaning to say, with one young in years, do not act thusly.[29] Rather, assume self-importance toward him and neither jest nor be familiar with him. Subsequently, he said, do not think that what I cautioned you against being familiar with one young in years would require that you greet him with indignation and with a sullen visage. Such is not the intention; rather, you should greet all men, small and great, free man and slave, every member of the human species, with cheerfulness. This exceeds what Shammai said, ". . . [*greet all men*] *with a pleasant countenance.*" [30]

The translator said, it appears to me from the master's words that he defines the word "m'kabel" from "hak-balath panim—greeting the presence," as if it (i.e.,

"m'kabel") were "makbil—greet [actively]," as derived from, "makbilloth halula'oth," for it (i.e., the meaning of the Hebrew word "makbilloth") is taken from the
Aramaic translation of "neged—opposite," or "nochaḥ
—before." [31] Thus regarding this subject as said in
the Arabic, the terminology for "meeting and greeting"
conveys: so and so met me with either cheerfulness or
sullenness. And here, through [its meaning in] that language, the master defined "m'kabel" [as "greet"]. Know
that this is so. [32]

> *XIII   Rabbi Akiba said: Jesting and levity condi-*
> *tion man to lewdness. The transmitted tradition is a*
> *fence to the Torah, tithes are a fence to riches,*
> *vows are a fence to separateness, a fence to wisdom*
> *is silence.*

XIII   When a man makes vows and fulfills them, he
will achieve the trait of absention from that of which
he wishes to abstain. That trait will become firm with
him, and *separateness* will be simple for him; [33] meaning to say, the vigilance of defilements, as they said in
Ḥagigah: [34] To the Pharisees, the clothes of an Am
Ha'aretz are imbued with treading-contact defilement.

> *XIV   He used to say: Beloved is man for he was*
> *created in the image. Greater is the love for*
> *it was made known to him that he was created in*
> *the image, as it is said, ". . . in the image of God*
> *He made man" (Genesis 9:6). Beloved are Israel*

for they are termed children of the Omnipres-
ent. Greater is the love for it was made known
to them that they are termed children of the Om-
nipresent, as it is said, "You are children of the Lord
your God. . . ." (Deuteronomy 14:1). Beloved
are Israel for a precious vessel was given to them.
Greater is the love for it was made known to
them that a precious vessel was given to them
through which the world was created, as it is said,
"For I give you good doctrine, forsake not My
Torah" (Proverbs 4:2).

XIV He used to say that making known the value of
the favor which they extended to him constitutes another
beneficence. For at times a man will bestow a favor upon
some other man by way of mercy, and he will not make
known to him the value of what he did for him because
he is contemptible in his sight.

XV   All is foreseen yet the authority is given, and
the world is judged by goodness, and everything is
[reckoned] according to the multitude of the deed.

XV This statement incorporates very important matters, and it is fitting that this statement be attributed to
Rabbi Akiba. This is its explanation in brief, and it is
offered on condition that you are aware of everything
that was previously stated in the introductory chapters.[35]
He said, everything that is in the world is known before
Him, may He be blessed, and He is conscious of it, as it

was said, *All is foreseen.* . . . Subsequently, he said, do not think that since He is cognizant of deeds that predetermination would be [logically] imperative; that is to say that man would be coerced in his deeds with regard to any deed. Such is not the case; rather, the authority is in the power of man in what he may do, as it was said, *yet the authority is given,* meaning to say that every man is given authority, as we explained in the Eighth Chapter.[36]

[With reference to . . . *and the world is judged by goodness.*] He said that the judgment of the Lord, may He be blessed, with men, is indeed through kindness and goodness, and not according to the judgment that is fitting for them. As the One to be blessed made clear from His ways, He said,[37] ". . . long-suffering and abundant in kindness and truth . . . ," and our Rabbis, may their memory be blessed, said: [38] Long-suffering to the righteous and to the wicked; and the prophet said,[39] "The Lord is good to all. . . ."

[With reference to . . . *and everything is [reckoned] according to the multitude of the deed.*] Subsequently, he said that virtues will not be attained by a man according to the magnitude of the deed, but according to the multitude of the number of the deeds. That is, that virtues will indeed be attained by repeating the good deeds many times. With this [method] he will attain a firm trait—and not when a man performs a single major act of the good acts, for through this alone he will not attain a firm trait. The illustration of this: When a man gives to one who is deserving a thousand gold pieces all at once, [that is,] to one man, and

he did not give anything to another man, he will not
achieve the attribute of generosity through this single
major deed, just as it is attained by one who contributed
a thousand gold pieces in a thousand instances, and gave
all of those gold pieces from the standpoint of generosity.
Inasmuch as this one repeated the practice of generosity a
thousand times, he attained a firm trait, whereas that one,
in only one instance was his soul powerfully stimulated
toward a good act, and thereafter it (i.e., the stimulus)
ceased from him. Thus, according to the Torah, the recompense for one who redeemed a captive for one hundred dinars, or dealt charitably toward a poor man to the
extent of one hundred dinars which was sufficient for his
need, is not on a par with the recompense for one who redeemed ten captives, or fulfilled the need of ten poor
men, each to the extent of ten dinars. It is with this
[illustration] that the analogy is made, and this is the
meaning of his statement, . . . *according to the multitude of the deed*, not, however, according to the magnitude of the deed.[40]

> *XVI He used to say: Everything is given on
> pledge and the net is spread over all the living. The
> shop is open, the shopkeeper extends credit, the
> ledger is open, the hand writes, and whoever desires
> to borrow let him come and borrow. The collectors
> make their round regularly every day, and they ex-
> act retribution from a man whether with his knowl-
> edge or without his knowledge. They have that
> upon which they can rely, the judgment is a judg-
> ment of truth, and everything is prepared for the
> banquet.*

XVI *The shopkeeper extends credit* [means] he who will prolong the collection of his debt and will not request it forthwith. This parable is clear and its intent is understood. His statement, . . . *and whoever desires to borrow let him come and borrow*, butresses the preceding subject, [namely,] that there is no predetermination there (i.e., before the Lord); rather, through man's choosing he will do what he may wish to do.[41] His statement, *The collectors make their round regularly*, is a parable concerning death and the rest of the punishments which come upon man. *And everything is prepared for the banquet*, that is to say, the ultimate of the intent of all this is the life of The World To Come.

> *XVII Rabbi Elazar ben Azariah said: If there is no Torah there is no proper conduct, and if there is no proper conduct there is no Torah. If there is no wisdom there is no fear, and if there is no fear there is no wisdom. If there is no knowledge there is no understanding, and if there is no understanding there is no knowledge. If there is no meal there is no Torah, and if there is no Torah there is no meal. He used to say: Everyone whose wisdom exceeds his deeds, to what is he like? To a tree whose branches are many and whose roots are few, the wind comes and uproots it and overturns it, as it is said, "For he shall be like a tamarisk in the desert and shall not see when good comes, but shall inherit the parched places of the wilderness, a salt land that is not inhabited" (Jeremiah 17:6). However, everyone whose deeds exceed his wisdom, to what is he like? To a tree whose branches are few*

*and whose roots are many, even if all the winds in
the world were to come and blow upon it, they
would not stir it from its place, as it is said, "For
he shall be like a tree planted by the water that
spreads its roots by the river, and shall not see
when heat comes, but its leaf shall be plentiful and
it will not be troubled in the year of drought nor
will it cease from yielding fruit" (Ibid., v. 8).*

XVII   By means of this he intends to say that [in]
each of these two, each one of the two avails in [bring-
ing about] the existence of the other, and completes
the other.

Concerning his teachings with regard to *knowledge*
and *understanding*—it is a very delicate philosophical
subject. I shall mention it relying upon the sagacity of
one who has reflected upon this subject. That is, the
knowledge which we attain and which we acquire indeed is our perceiving ideas which we perceive by ab-
stracting the form, and we will then apprehend it (i.e.,
the idea); or, we may perceive abstract forms in their
subjective existence without our transforming them into
knowledge; they, however, in their subjective existence
represent knowledge. This perception is what would be
termed *understanding*, and it constitutes *knowledge*.
Through knowledge we may also comprehend, and it is
then possible for us that we perceive what we may perceive. It is as if he said: If we will not apprehend the idea
we have no knowledge, and if we will not have knowledge we will not apprehend the idea, for it is through
knowledge that we perceive it. The comprehension of

this matter is very difficult, even from the books that were authored on it—certainly from here. However, we only direct the straight path through it.[42]

Everyone whose deeds; we have explained and clarified these words in this chapter through the teachings of Rabbi Ḥanina ben Dosa [43]

> *XVIII   Rabbi Elazar ben Ḥisma said: [The laws regarding] bird-offerings and the onset of menstruation indeed are essential laws. Astronomy and geometry are after-courses of wisdom.*

XVIII   This is clear. We have elucidated its meaning in the introductory chapters.[44]

4

1   Ben Zoma said: Who is wise? One who learns from all men, as it is said, "From all my teachers I have obtained understanding. . . ." (Psalms 119:99). Who is mighty? One who subdues his inclination, as it is said, "He who is slow to anger is better than the mighty, and he who rules his spirit than he who takes a city" (Proverbs 16:32). Who is rich? One who rejoices in his portion, as it is said, "When you eat of the labor of your hands you shall be happy and it shall be well with you" (Psalms 128:2). "You shall be happy"—in this world, "and

it shall be well with you"—in The World To Come.
Who is honored? One who honors mankind, as it is
said, ". . . for those who honor Me I will honor,
and those who despise Me will be lightly esteemed"
(I Samuel 2:30).

I   This is clear. We have mentioned its meaning in the
introductory chapters.[1]

> *II   Ben Azzai said: Be swift to fulfil a light precept*
> *even as one would a weighty one, and flee from*
> *transgression. For precept leads to precept and*
> *transgression leads to transgression. For the recom-*
> *pense of a precept is a precept, and the recompense*
> *of a transgression is a transgression.*

II   We have clarified the explanation of this statement
in the tenth chapter of Sanhedrin.[2] The sages, peace
be upon them, have disclosed a remarkable new point in
the Torah which contains stimulus for practicing the precepts. As it was said,[3] "Then Moses set apart three
cities across the Jordan . . . ," it was known that they
would not avail inasmuch as the law of the cities of
refuge would not be applicable in them until the other
three in the land of Israel were set apart. They said: [4]
Moses our master, peace be upon him, was aware that the
three cities in Trans-Jordan would not afford asylum
until the three in the land of Israel were set apart, as it is
said,[5] ". . . there shall be six cities of refuge." However,
he set these apart because he said, "Since a precept has
come into my power, I will fulfill it." [6] If it was as this

manner with Moses our master, peace be upon him, the perceiver of truths, the perfect of the perfect, who yearned to add one-half a positive precept to all his virtue and perfection, it goes without saying that they whose souls are leprous, and whose leprosy has become firm and has advanced, should practice [the precepts].[7]

> *III   He used to say: Do not scorn any man and do not regard any thing as impossible, for there is no man who has not his hour and not a thing which has not its place.*

III   He said that it is impossible that there will not be a time for any man in which he could either harm or aid, even in a trifling matter.

> *IV   Rabbi Levitas of Jabneh said: Be exceedingly humble in spirit, for the expectation of man is the worm. Rabbi Joḥanan ben Beroka said: Whoever profanes the name of Heaven in secret, they exact retribution from him openly. Unwitting and witting are as one with regard to profanation of the Name.*

IV   In the introductory chapters we have explained and noted that modesty is of the moral virtues, and it is midway between pride and humbleness of spirit, and it has no other appellation except "modesty." [8] Pride, however, has many appellations in the Hebrew language: "arrogant," "conceited," "proud," and "exalted."

Of the appellations applied by the sages, may their memory be blessed: "insolent," "haughty," and "overbearing." [9] Over against them is "humbleness of spirit."

In the Fourth Chapter we have explained that, from the standpoint of a precautionary measure, a man should incline a bit toward one of the extremes so that he will stand at the median of deeds.[10] However, only with regard to this attribute among the rest of the attributes, meaning to say, in the instance of pride, due to the magnitude of the shortcoming of this attribute according to the saintly, and because of their awareness of its detriment, they removed from it until the extreme of deficiency, and they inclined completely to humbleness of spirit in order that they would not leave any room for pride in their souls.[11]

I have seen in a certain book from among the books on ethics where it was asked of one of the esteemed saintly men—it was said to him, "Of all your days, in which day did you most rejoice?" He said: On the day that I was traveling on a ship, and my place was in the lowliest of the places on the ship, [that is,] amongst the bundles of clothes.[12] On the ship were merchants and wealthy men. I was lying in my place and one of the men on the ship arose to urinate. I was insignificant and contemptible in his sight because in his sight I was very low, until he uncovered his nakedness and urinated on me. I was astonished at the firmness of the disposition of brazeness in his soul. As the Lord lives, my soul was not pained at his deed at all, nor was my power [to react in anger] aroused within me. Instead, I re-

joiced greatly when I attained the limit where the contempt of that deficient man did not pain me and
that my soul was not stirred up toward him. There is
no doubt that this is the ultimate of humbleness of spirit
—in order that one may remove from pride.

I shall now mention part of what the sages noted in
praise of modesty and in denunciation of pride. Accordingly, he exhorted us to draw near to humbleness and
said, *Be exceedingly humble in spirit*—out of his concern
that man would remain only within [the mean of]
modesty.[13] [For if he were to remain only within the
mean of modesty,] there would certainly be a bit of
pride in him since it (i.e., the extreme of pride) is near
to it (i.e., the mean of modesty), since modesty, as
we noted, is midway.[14]

In praise of modesty they said: [15] What wisdom
made into a crown for its head, modesty made into a
heel ("akayv") for its sole, meaning, for its boot. As
it is written,[16] "Fear of the Lord is the beginning of
wisdom . . . ," this is the proof that fear of the Lord
is greater than wisdom and it is the cause of its existence.
And he said,[17] "As a consequence ("aykev") of modesty, fear of the Lord [will ensue] . . . ," that is to say
that fear of the Lord will be found in the train of modesty. This being so, modesty is much greater than wisdom.[18]

They said: [19] This subject is written in the Torah,
repeated in the Prophets, and repeated a third time in
the Hagiographa; [20] wherever you find the greatness of
the Holy One, blessed be He, there you find His modesty. It is written in the Torah,[21] ". . . the great God,

[the mighty and the awesome . . . ,]" and following this it is written,[22] "Who executes justice for the orphan and the widow. . . ." It is repeated in the Prophets, as it is written,[23] "For thus said the High and Lofty One that inhabits eternity and whose name is Holy, I abide in the high and holy place . . . ," and alongside it,[24] ". . . with him that is of a contrite and humble spirit. . . ." It is repeated a third time in the Hagiographa, as it is written,[25] ". . . extol Him that traverses the skies, whose name is the Lord . . . ," and following this it is written,[26] "A father of the orphans and a judge of the widows. . . ."

You are required to learn from Moses our master, peace be upon him, in whom the intellectual virtues and the moral virtues were perfected, and all of them were directed toward the zenith of prophecy.[27] [He was] foremost in the Torah, foremost in wisdom, and foremost in prophecy, and the Lord, may He be blessed, praised him above all men for the attribute of modesty, and He said,[28] "And the man Moses was very modest above all men. . . ." His saying "very" signifies the excessiveness of his modesty and of his inclining toward the side of the extreme of deficiency; [29] thus, you find him saying,[30] ". . . and what are we. . . ."

Thus in the instance of David, the anointed of the God of Jacob and the sweet singer of Israel; he is an honored king whose kingdom became great, whose sword waxed mighty, and whom the Lord, may He be blessed, promised to us through Moses our master, peace be upon him—he is the star which stepped forth out of Jacob,[31] as our Rabbis, may their memory be blessed, explained,[32] and he is a prophet and the greatest of the seventy elders, as it was said,[33] ". . . who sits as the counsellor at the academy." Nevertheless, he said,[34] ". . . a broken and contrite heart God will not despise." There are many of these virtues which denote the ultimate of modesty.[35]

From what our Rabbis, may their memory be blessed, said with regard to pride, their saying: [36] Every man who has haughtiness is as if he worships an idol; here it is written,[37] "Whoever is arrogant is an abomination of the Lord . . . ," and there it is written,[38] "And you shall not bring an abomination into your house. . . ." And they said: [39] It is as if he denied the fundamental principle, as it is said,[40] "Then your heart be lifted up and you forget the Lord. . . ."

They said: [41] [One who is guilty of] the sin of pride is as he who transgresses the laws of incestuous relationships; it said,[42] "Whoever is arrogant is an abomination of the Lord . . . ," and it said [with regard to incestuous relationships],[43] "For all these abominations. . . ."

They said: [44] According to the Lord, may He be blessed, the overbearing one himself is as an idol itself, and they adduced proof from the statement,[45] "Cease you from the man in whose nostrils is a breath . . . ," that is to say, the insolent,[46] ". . . for how little ("bameh") is he to be reckoned," [47] read not, "bameh—how little," but "bamah—idolatrous altar." [48]

They said, the overbearing is worthy of execution, [as is indicated] when they said: [49] Everyone who has haughtiness is worthy of being cut down as an Asherah; here it is written,[50] ". . . and the high ones of stature will be cut down . . . ," and there it is written,[51] ". . . and you shall cut down their Asherim. . . ."

They said that the Lord, may He be blessed, will not revivify the overbearing in The Revivification of The Dead,[52] [as is indicated] when they said: [53] Every man who has haughtiness, his dust will not be stirred, as it is said,[54] ". . . awake and sing you that dwell in the dust . . . ," [meaning,] he who in his lifetime became as dust, meaning to say, the modest, they are the ones who will be revivified. They hyperbolized with regard to this, and they said: [55] Every man who has haughtiness, the Divine Presence bewails him, as it is said,[56] ". . . and the lofty one He knows from afar."

And [there are] many of their teachings [in a similar vein; as an example], when they said that leprosy is the punishment for the overbearing. They said: [57] "And for a rising and for a scab and for a bright spot"—"a rising" refers to aught but the lofty one, as it is said,[58] ". . . and upon all the hills that are lifted up"; it is as if it said, "To the overbearing—the scab."

In concluding they said: [59] He who possesses [pride] deserves excommunication, and he who does not possess any deserves excommunication; meaning to say that it is not proper for man to be of absolute humble spirit, because it is not of the virtues. By way of an illustration they conjectured it: one sixty-fourth part, meaning to say, when we place pride at one extreme and humbleness of spirit at the other extreme, there will be a width between them of sixty-four parts, [meaning,] that a man should stand at the sixty-third part.[60] He does not approve of the middle course only with regard to this attribute—in order to flee from pride.[61] For if he were to lack one part and would draw that much closer to pride, he will enter under [the sentence of] excommunication. This was Rabba's opinion with regard to modesty.

Rabbi Naḥman, however, offered the deciding statement. He said: It is not proper for man to have of it, meaning to say, of pride, neither a great part nor a small part, for its sin is not that trifling that it should make a man into an "abomination of the Lord." [62] Therefore, it is not proper to draw near to it. With reference to this subject, Rabbi Naḥman bar Isaac said: [63] Neither it nor part of it, for is it a trifling matter concerning which it is written,[64] "Whoever is arrogant is an abomination of the Lord . . . !"

Due to the severity of this accursed sin, he said, *Be exceedingly humble in spirit for the expectation of man is the worm*, meaning to say, you are required to compel your soul so that pride will be removed from it through your contemplating the future of the body, that is, its becoming worm.

[With reference to *Unwitting and witting are as one with regard to profanation of the Name*.] You are aware from Scripture that the unwitting bears sin, consequently, he requires atonement through an offering.[65] The Lord, may He be blessed, said concerning him,[66] ". . . and he shall be forgiven for his sin which he had sinned," however, he is not like the witting.[67] Far be it from the Righteous in His Way, the Lord, may He be blessed, to equate the witting and the unwitting in any matter;[68] rather, his intention here [is to teach as follows]: In the case of profanation of the Name, whether it were witting or unwitting, they exact retribution from him openly.[69] If he were witting, the punishment is that due the witting; if he were unwitting, the punishment is that due the unwitting. Both punishments, however, are exacted openly.

> *V Rabbi Ishmael [his son] said: One who learns in order to teach is afforded the opportunity to learn and to teach. Whereas one who learns in order to practice is afforded the opportunity to learn, to teach, to observe, and to practice. Rabbi Zadok said: Do not fashion it into a crown with which to magnify yourself, nor into a spade with which to dig. Thus Hillel used to say, "And he who makes use of the crown will perish." Hence you may deduce; whoever derives benefit from the words of the Torah removes his life from the world.*

V After I decided that I would not discuss this counsel because it is clear, and also because of my awareness that my teachings concerning it would not appeal to most of the great sages of the Torah, and perhaps to all of them, I revoked my decision and I shall discuss it without regard to either previous or current authorities.[70]

Know that this which he said, "that you shall not fashion the Torah into a spade with which to dig," is to say, do not consider it an implement with which to earn a livelihood;[71] and he explained and said that everyone who will derive benefit in this world through the honor of the Torah removes his life from the world, meaning, from the life of The World To Come.[72] People distorted this obvious language and they cast it (i.e., the correct meaning) behind their backs, and they depended upon the literal meanings of the words, for they did not understand them, therefore, I shall explain them.

They established portions for themselves which devolved upon individuals and upon communities, and by means of utter folly they brought people to think that this is obligatory, and that it is proper that they aid scholars and students and men who are engaged in the Torah and for whom the Torah represents their craft. All this is in error. We will not find in the Torah nor in the teachings of the sages a teaching which will verify it, nor a basis upon which it will be supported at all.

For were we to reflect upon the teachings of our Rabbis, may their memory be blessed, with regard to them we will not find that they requested money from people, nor did they collect money for honored and esteemed academies, nor for Exilarchs, nor for their judges, nor for disseminators of the Torah, nor for any of the great, nor for the rest of the people of the folk.[73] Instead, we will find in every generation, in all their communities, that among them there were poor in the extreme of poverty, as well as very wealthy in the extreme of wealth. Far be it from me to suspect those generations that they were not kind and charitable. For indeed, had that poor man stretched forth his hand to take, they would have filled his house with gold and pearls, but he was unwilling. Instead, he was content with his work through which he was supported, whether in abundance or in scarcity, and he spurned what people possessed because the Torah precluded him from this.

You are aware that Hillel the Elder was a wood hewer and he used to study under Shemaiah and Abtalyon, and he was poor in the extreme of poverty.[74] His station was pre-eminent as you are aware from his disciples who were compared to Moses, Aaron, and Joshua, and the least significant among his disciples was Rabbi Johanan ben Zakkai.[75] The discerning have no doubt that, had he instructed the people of his generation [that it was proper for him] to derive benefit from them, they would not have allowed him to hew wood. And Rabbi Ḥanina ben Dosa for whom a Heavenly Voice went forth and proclaimed, "The entire world is sustained only because of My son Ḥanina, and as for My son Ḥanina, he is satisfied with a kab of carobs from one Sabbath eve to the next," and he did not request from people.[76] And Karna was a judge in the land of Israel and he was a water drawer.[77] When litigants would come before him he used to say, "Give me one who will draw water in my place," or, "Give me [an amount] sufficient for [the loss incurred by] my idleness and I will judge for you." [78]

The Israelites of their generation were neither cruel nor unkind. Nor do we find a sage of the needy sages who denounced the people of his generation because they did not enrich them. Far be it from them. Instead, they themselves were saintly men, believers in the truth for its own sake, and they believed in the Lord, may He be blessed, and in the Torah of Moses through which man will merit the life of The World To Come, and they did not allow themselves to request money from people. They understood that taking it constituted a profanation of the Name in the sight of the multitude, inasmuch as they would think that the Torah is merely another trade through which a man may earn a livelihood, and it would be despised in their sight, thus he who does this ". . . contemned the word of the Lord. . . ." [79]

Indeed, those who are bold to dispute the truth and the plain passages, and who are overt in taking people's money either with their consent or against their consent, have led astray by means of the incidents that will be found in the Gemara regarding persons who are bodily impaired, or regarding elderly people who are advanced in years so that it is impossible for them to perform work. For they have no recourse but to take money from others; for if not, what shall they do—are they to die? The Torah did not command this.

You will find that the incident from which they adduced proof when they said,[80] "She is like the merchant ships, she brings her food from afar," refers to a physically impaired person who is unable to perform work; however, with the capability, the Torah did not afford him the means [with which he could justify accepting a gift].[81] Rabbi Joseph conveyed wood from place to place and he used to say,[82] "Great is work for it warms those who perform it," meaning to say, with the travail of his limbs, for while he carried the heavy wood he

would undoubtedly warm his body. He used to praise
this and rejoice in it, and he derived pleasure in what the
Lord, may He be blessed, apportioned to him for he possessed of the virtue of contentedness.[83]

I have heard the simpletons who are dependent upon
proofs which they adduced, when they said: [84] One
who desires to derive benefit may derive benefit as
Elisha, and one who desires not to derive benefit let him
not derive benefit as Samuel the Ramahthite. [The meaning of] this [statement] is not at all similar to that which
they adduce. However, in my opinion it is a major dis-
tortion to adduce proof from it, because it is clear and
it is not an area where a man might err in it. For Elisha
would not accept money from people—he would certainly not request of them and establish portions which
devolved upon them. Heaven forbid! Rather, he would
merely be accepting respect when a man would give him
lodging when he passed his way by staying with him in
his house, and he would eat of his food on that night or
on that day and would then return to his affairs.[85]
Samuel, however, would neither enter a man's house
nor would he eat with any man. Stemming from this,
the sages, may their memory be blessed, said: [86] When
a scholar wishes to emulate him, so that he would
not enter a man's house, the authority is in his power;
if he wishes to lodge with a man when he passed
his way for the necessity of carrying out a journey, the
authority is in his power, for they have cautioned
against eating at any man's except if there be a necessity.[87] They said: [88] The scholar who increases taking

his meals in all places [will inevitably suffer great harm]. And they said: [89] Any meal that is not associated with a precept, it is forbidden for a scholar to derive benefit from it.

Why need I prolong with regard to this subject? However, I shall mention the incident that was clearly related in the Gemara, [and my reason for doing so will become apparent].[90] That is, a certain man had a vineyard which thieves used to enter. In every instance in which he would observe it daily, he would find its fruits constantly diminishing. He had no doubt that one of the thieves had set his eye on it, and he was distressed because of this all the days of the vintage, until he gathered from it what he gathered, and set them out to dry until they dried, then he gathered the raisins. As is usual with people when they gather raisins, seeds from the [dried] figs and from the grapes will fall from them (i.e., the gatherers), and it is permitted to eat them because they are ownerless, and the property owners have left them to their finders because of their trifling number. One day Rabbi Tarfon came upon that vineyard by chance. He sat down, gathered of the raisins that had fallen, and was eating them. Along came the owner of the vineyard and he thought that this was the thief who stole from him all through the year—he did not recognize him but had heard of him—he immediately took hold of him, overpowered him, put him into a sack, put him over his back, and was about to throw him into a river. When Rabbi Tarfon understood thus, he cried out and said, "Woe to Tarfon that this one is about to kill him." When the owner of the vineyard heard [the name Tarfon], he put him down and fled —because of his awareness that he had committed a great sin. Rabbi Tarfon was distressed from that day and thenceforward all his days, and he grieved over what had happened to him for he had rescued himself through the honor of the Torah. Since he was a very rich man, he could have said, "Put me down and I will give you such and such an amount of gold pieces," and he would have given them to him and would not have had to make known that he was Rabbi Tarfon, and would have rescued himself by means of his money and not by means of the Torah. They said: Throughout all the days of this righteous man he was distressed over this matter, and he said, "Woe to me that I made use of the crown of the Torah," for all who make use of the crown of the Torah have no share in The World To Come and are uprooted from the world. They said this because Rabbi Tarfon was a very rich man and he should have appeased him with money.[91]

Thus Rabbenu HaKaddosh, peace be upon him, opened storehouses in a year of famine, and declared,[92] "Everyone who wishes to come and to take his sustenance, let him come and be supported, provided that he be a Talmid Ḥacham." [93] Rabbi Jonathan ben Amram came and stood before him, and he (i.e., Rabbi Judah HaNasi) did not recognize him. He said to him, "Rabbi, support me." He said to him, "Have you studied Bible?" —"No." "Have you studied Mishnah?"—"No." "Through what shall I support you?" He said to him, "Support me as a dog or as a raven," meaning to say, even though there is no wisdom in me, [support me] just as the Lord, may He be blessed, would support an unclean animal or an unclean bird, for an Am Ha'aretz is not less significant than them, and he gave him.[94] Afterwards, he regretted [having supported him] because he had persuaded him with his words, and he said, "Woe to me that an Am Ha'aretz has derived benefit from my possessions." Those who heard what had happened to him said to him, "Perhaps he is your disciple Jonathan ben Amram who does not wish to derive benefit through the honor of the Torah when he could guard against this, even by means of a subterfuge." He investigated and found the matter to be so. These two incidents will silence all who are disputatious with regard to this subject.[95]

Concerning the matters which the Torah permitted for scholars—that is, they may give their money to a man in order to engage in business with according to his choosing, and if he wishes, the entire profit will be theirs. One who does this has a great recompense because of it;[96] this is "casting merchandise to the scholar's account."[97] Their goods should be sold before any goods, and they (i.e., the merchants) should sell to them at the beginning of the market.[98] These are the portions which the Lord, may He be blessed, established for them according to what is mentioned in the tradition,[99] just as He established the portions for the Priest and the tithes for the Levite.[100] As for these two practices, the merchants should arrange them one with another by way of respect, even though there is no wisdom there; for a scholar is deserving of being on a par with a respected ignoramus.[101]

Thus the Torah relieved scholars of crop taxes, quartering of armies, and the taxes which specifically apply to each and every man, they are what are termed "poll tax." [In each of these instances] the community would pay for them. Similarly, [in the case of taxes levied for] the construction of walls, and matters of the like.[102] Even if the scholar were a wealthy man, he would not owe a thing regarding all this. Rabbi Joseph HaLevi, may his memory be blessed, ruled concerning a man in a certain place who had gardens and orchards and who owed thousands of gold pieces for them. He said that he should be exempt from giving a thing for them regarding all that we mentioned because he was a scholar, although even the poorest Israelite would give for that levy.[103] This is a law of the Torah, just as the Torah exempted the priests from the half-shekel, as we explained in its place, and matters that are similar to this.[104]

> *VI   Rabbi Jose said: Whoever honors the Torah is himself honored by mankind. Whereas whoever dishonors the Torah is himself dishonored by mankind.*

VI   The honor of the Torah, that is, when one displays zealousness in practicing it, and he will honor the sages who sustain it and the books which they authored on it. Thus, dishonoring the Torah is the opposite of the three.

> *VII   Rabbi Ishmael, his son, said: One who withholds himself from judgment rids himself of en-*

mity, theft, and perjury. One who is presumptuous in rendering decision is foolish, wicked, and haughty.

VII   In rendering decision he is presumptuous, [that is,] to be bold to render decision without fear or anxiety.

VIII   He used to say: Do not judge alone, for there is none who may judge alone save One. And do not say, "accept my opinion," for it is for them to choose and not you.

VIII   The Torah permitted a man who is a publicly acknowledged expert to judge alone, as we explained in Sanhedrin. However, this [allowance] is a teaching of the Torah, and he partly cautioned against it here from the standpoint of ethics and not from the standpoint of a prohibition.[105]

He said, when your colleagues disagree with you in any matter of opinion, do not compel them to accept your reasoning. For they discern whether they are required to accept it, and it is not within your authority to compel them to accept your opinion.

IX   Rabbi Jonathan said: Whoever fulfills the Torah when poor will in the end fulfill it when wealthy. Whereas whoever neglects the Torah when wealthy will in the end neglect it when poor.

IX He said, one who engages in the Torah while he is poor and needy, and nevertheless will trouble himself to engage in it, in the end he shall engage in it when wealthy and when he will not have anything that will hinder him from study. Whereas he who will not engage in the Torah owing to an abundance of wealth and consequently is occupied with food, with drink, and with pleasure, will in the end become poor and fortune will place him in straitened circumstances so that his preoccupation with food for his meal will be the reason for his neglect of study.[106]

X Rabbi Meir said: Lessen business affairs and engage in the Torah, and be humble of spirit before all men. If you have neglected the Torah, there will be many idle things before you. However, if you have toiled in the Torah, there is a great recompense to be given to you.

X He said, lessen business activities and be constant in the Torah.

And be humble of spirit before all men, meaning to say, do not be humble of spirit only before the great. Rather, [be humble of spirit] before all men, so that when you sit with any man that it may be, let your conversation with him be as if he is greater in rank than yourself—all this in order to flee from pride, as we explained.[107]

The meaning of *there will be many idle things before you* is that there are many matters which cause neglect [of study], and they will be required of one who is engaged in them. When you do not engage in the Torah, fortune will preoccupy you with one of those matters.[108]

> XI   *Rabbi Eliezer ben Jacob said: One who per-*
> *forms one precept acquires an advocate for him-*
> *self. Whereas one who commits one transgres-*
> *sion acquires an accuser for himself. Repentance*
> *and good deeds are as a shield against retribution.*
> *Rabbi Joḥanan ha'Sandelar said: Every assem-*
> *bly that is convened for the sake of Heaven will*
> *in the end endure. Whereas that which is not con-*
> *vened for the sake of Heaven will in the end not*
> *endure.*

XI   *Advocate* is one who intercedes in favor of a man before the ruler. *Accuser* is the opposite of this; he is one who calumniates a man before the king and attempts to have him put to death.

He said that repentance after evil deeds, or good deeds [performed] at the outset of the case, each of these two conditions preclude afflictions and illnesses from coming upon man.

> XII   *Rabbi Elazar ben Shammua said: Let the*
> *honor of your disciple be as dear to you as your*
> *own, and the honor of your colleague as the fear*
> *of your teacher, and the fear of your teacher as*
> *the fear of Heaven. Rabbi Judah said: Be cautious*
> *in study, for an unwitting error in study is consid-*

ered witting error. Rabbi Simeon said: There are
three crowns—the crown of the Torah, the crown
of the priesthood, and the crown of the kingship,
but the crown of a good name exceeds them all.

XII   These three excellent ranks were given to this
nation at the outset with the giving of the Torah. They
are the priesthood, the kingship, and the Torah. Priesthood was merited by Aaron, kingship was merited by
David, but the crown of the Torah is set aside for everyone who wishes to be crowned with it.[109] Our Rabbis,
may their memory be blessed, said: [110] You might say
that this crown is less significant than the other two—
this is not so. Rather, it is greater than both of them,
and through it the two will come about, as it is said,[111]
"By me kings reign and princes decree justice," and it
said, "By me princes rule. . . ." However, the crown
of a good name is attained through the Torah, meaning
to say, the knowledge of it and the practice of it, for
through them the true good name will be attained.

XIII   Rabbi Nehorai said: Transport yourself to a
place of Torah, and do not say that it will follow
you. For it will endure as yours through study with
your colleagues, and do not rely upon your under-
standing.

XIII   He said, seek the place of study and learning.
For with someone else study will be made possible for
you and it will endure. Do not rely upon your sagacity

and say that you do not require colleagues and students
to bestir you.

> *XIV   Rabbi Jannai said: We have not the power
> to explain either the tranquility of the wicked or
> the chastisements of the righteous. Rabbi Mattithiah
> ben Ḥeresh said: Be first in extending greeting to
> all men; be a tail to lions and do not be a head to
> foxes.*[112]

XIV   [With reference to *Be a tail to lions. . . .*] He
said, when a man is a student to one who is wiser than
he, it is more beneficial to him, and it is more suitable
than his being a teacher to one of lesser stature than he.
For in the first condition he will increase, and in the second condition he will decrease. You will understand
from what we explained in Sanhedrin, that based on the
reason, "In matters of sanctity we elevate and we do
not lower," they installed the head of the court of
twenty-three at the end [position] of the seventy-one
of the great court, for they understood that through this
they added rank to him.[113]

> *XVI   Rabbi Jacob said: This world is like a vesti-
> bule before The World To Come. Prepare your-
> self in the vestibule that you may enter the banquet
> hall.*

XVI   *Banquet hall* refers to the palace, and *Vestibule*
refers to the gate-house. The parable is clear and the

intent is understood, that in this world a man may acquire the virtues through which he will merit The
World To Come. For in truth, this world is a path and
a crossing to The World To Come.

> *XVII He used to say: Better is one hour of re-*
> *pentance and good deeds in this world than all the*
> *life of The World To Come. Better is one hour of*
> *serenity in The World To Come than all the life*
> *of this world.*

XVII In the tenth chapter of Sanhedrin we have explained that after death there is neither perfection nor
addition; [114] rather, man will achieve perfection and add
virtue in this world. Solomon alluded to this when he
said,[115] ". . . for there is no work, nor device, nor
knowledge, nor wisdom, in the grave to which you go."
However, that state in which man departs will remain
with him for eternity. Therefore, man needs to be diligent in this short time and should only expend his time
in aught but the acquisition of virtues; for his loss is great,
since he does not have either substitution or remedy. Because the saintly were cognizant of this, they considered
it proper to consume it only in [the pursuit of] wisdom
and in the addition of virtues. They invested all their
time in the correct path, and they squandered only a
very small amount of time in sensual matters and in
the necessary matter that is impossible to do without.
Whereas others spent all their time only in sensual matters, and they departed from it in the same manner that
they came, [as it is said,] [116] ". . . in all points as he

came, so shall he go . . . ," and they forfeited it all as
an eternal forfeiture.

The entire multitude reverses the truth with regard
to this question and they say that the former group forfeited the world, and that the latter group gained the
world.[117] As we related, the case is the opposite. They,
however, make darkness into light and light into darkness, woe to them that cause the truth to perish.[118]
Solomon, peace be upon him, made this subject a fundamental point in Ecclesiastes when he praised the gain
of The World [To Come] and denounced its forfeiture,
and made it clear that there is neither gain nor acquisition after death beyond the matter which one withheld
from [attaining] here.[119] All this is true; when you
examine that book with this point of view the truth will
become clear.

> *XVIII   Rabbi Simeon ben Elazar said: Do not
> soothe your fellow in the hour of his anger, do not
> console him in the hour when his dead lies before
> him, do not question him in the hour of his vow,
> and do not attempt to see him in the hour of his
> disgrace.*

XVIII   This is clear. They are ethical qualities concerning improvement of man's social relations and regarding
casting the word in its advantageous place.

> *XIX   Samuel the Younger said: "Rejoice not when
> your enemy falls, and let your heart not be glad
> when he stumbles. Lest the Lord see it and be evil*

in His sight and He turn away His wrath from him" (*Proverbs 24:17–8*).

XIX   It is not said, "His fierce wrath," but "His wrath," which teaches that he is forgiven for all his sins.[120] Although it was Solomon in his wisdom who stated this counsel, nevertheless, this sage used to reprove [with it] for this attribute and caution against this transgression.[121]

> *XX   Elisha ben Abuyah said: One who learns when young, to what is he like? To ink written on new paper. One who learns when old, to what is he like? To ink written on paper that has been erased. Rabbi Jose bar Judah of K'far HaBabli said: One who learns from the young, to what is he like? To one who eats unripe grapes and drinks wine from his winepress. One who learns from the old, to what is he like? To one who eats ripe grapes and drinks old wine. Rabbi said: Look not at the jug, but at what is in it. There may be a new jug filled with old wine and an old jug that has not even new wine in it.*

XX   [With reference to *One who learns when young. . . .*] He said that what one learns in the period of youth will endure and it will not be easily forgotten, and the case with regard to what one learns in the period of old age is the opposite. This is clear and is apparent to the inner eye.

[With reference to *One who learns from the young.*

. . .] Rabbi Jose said that the wisdom of youths contains questions and doubts that are unsettled. Nor have they been spared from problems inasmuch as they have not lived long enough to repeat their learning and to remove doubts.

[With reference to *Look not at the jug.* . . .] Rabbi said, do not examine the wine by its jug; for there may be a new jug that contains old wine, and an old, empty jug that has not a thing in it. Thus there may be youths whose questions and wisdom are pure and are not mingled with doubt, [they are] like old wine whose lees have been separated from it. [Similarly,] there may be elders who have no wisdom at all, there being no need to state that they do not have mingled and confused wisdom.

> *XXI   Rabbi Elazar HaKappar said: Envy, lust, and ambition remove a man from the world.*

XXI   He said, envy, lust, and love of honor remove a man from the world. That is, by means of these attributes, or through one of them, he will perforce impair belief in the Torah and he will not attain either intellectual virtues or moral virtues.

> *XXII   He used to say: Those who have been born are to die. Those who have died are to be revivified. Those who have been revivified are to be judged. To know, to make known, and to be made aware that He is God, He is the Fashioner, He is the Creator, He is the Discerner, He is the Judge, He*

is the Witness, He is the Complainant, and He is
destined to judge, blessed be He, before whom
there is neither unrighteousness, nor forgetfulness,
nor regarding of persons, nor taking of bribes, for
all is His. And know that all is according to the
reckoning. And let not your imagination cause you
to trust that the netherworld will be a refuge for
you. For not of your will were you fashioned, not
of your will were you born, not of your will do
you live, not of your will do you die, and not of
your will are you destined to give an account and
reckoning before the King of kings, the Holy One,
blessed be He.

XXII   He said, *To know, to make known, and to be*
made aware . . . ; meaning thereby, that He is cognizant of those who are destined to be born, and of those
who are at this time born (i.e., currently alive), which
will die, and which will be revivified after death. We
deduce from [His having cognizance of] these three
groups that *He is the Fashioner,* and *He is the Creator.*

And his statement, *He is the Judge . . . and He is*
destined to judge . . . ; meaning thereby, that He at
this time judges all with regard to life and with regard
to death as well as the rest of mundane matters, and
He is also destined to judge those who will be revivified
for The World To Come with regard to reward and
punishment.[122]

He said, *nor taking of bribes.* It is similar to that
which was also stated in the Torah,[123] ". . . who does
not regard persons nor take a bribe." It does not mean

that He will not take a bribe in order to pervert justice, for this is a matter of folly to have removed from the Lord, may He be blessed, what cannot be imagined and certainly cannot be conceived. For how could bribery be imagined concerning Him? What would the bribe be? However, its meaning is what we explained: [124] He will not take good deeds as a bribe. As in the instance where a man will perform a thousand good deeds and one evil deed, the Lord, may He be blessed, will not forgive that transgression because of the multitude of his good deeds by deducting one or more good deeds for him from his thousand good deeds. Rather, he will be punished for that single evil deed and He will reward him for all those good deeds. That is the meaning of ". . . nor take a bribe." And it is similar to ". . . who does not regard persons . . . ," [which means] that He will punish one who is great in virtues for a minor matter, just as Moses our master, peace be upon him, was punished for the sin of anger, as we explained in the introductory chapters.[125] [Similarly, we note] the reward of Esau the wicked for honoring father and mother, and Nebuchadnezzar for honoring the Lord, may He be blessed, as was made clear in Sanhedrin.[126] That is the meaning of *nor regarding of persons. . . .*

Examine the statement, *not of your will were you born . . .* and what was conjoined to it. For he mentioned natural matters where man has no choice concerning them, since with regard to them, our Rabbis, may their memory be blessed, said: [127] Everything is in the power of Heaven except the fear of Heaven. And he did not say, "and not of your will do you sin," or "transgress," or "walk," or "stand," or anything that is similar to this; for all these are matters that are within man's authority and there is no predetermination in them, as we explained in the Eighth Chapter.[128]

1 With ten utterances the world was created. What is taught thereby? Could it not have been created with one utterance? However, this was taught in order to exact retribution from the wicked who destroy the world which was created with ten utterances, and in order to give an excellent recompense to the righteous who maintain the world which was created with ten utterances.

I When you consider all that was mentioned in the cosmogony, you will find that "va'yomer—and . . .

92

said," occurs nine times, and "B'reshith—In the beginning," represents the tenth [utterance].¹ Although the word "va'yomer" was not explicitly stated in it (i.e., the first act of creation), the subject denotes it, and it is as if it said, "And God said let there be heaven and earth," for they could not have come into being without an utterance. Yet it could have recounted the entire creation with one utterance by saying, "And God said let there be heaven and earth, let there be a firmament, let the waters be gathered," and so on. However, it singled out an utterance for each aspect in order to make known the greatness of this existence and the excellence of its order, and that one who corrupts it impairs a thing of great importance, and that one who improves it rectifies a thing of great importance. "One who corrupts it," meaning to say, "he who corrupts his soul," for it is within his power to improve it or to corrupt it,² and it is as if it is the ultimate purpose of all existence concerning which ten utterances were stated, as we explained in our introduction to this treatise.³

> II   *Ten generations from Adam to Noah [are enumerated] in order to make known the extent of His long-suffering, for all the generations provoked Him continually until He brought upon them the waters of the flood. Ten generations from Noah to Abraham [are enumerated] in order to make known the extent of His long-suffering, for all the generations provoked Him continually until Abraham our father came and received the recompense of them all.*

II   These generations are statements of the Torah—
"So and so begot so and so" following in sequence.[4] He
mentioned this [Mishnah] and that which follows it
since he had mentioned [the Mishnah of] "Ten Utterances," for through them moral instruction is given to
·man to stimulate him and to improve his soul by means of
the moral virtues and the intellectual virtues. For this is
the purpose of this tractate.[5]

*III   Abraham our father was tried with ten trials
and he withstood them all, in order to make known
the extent of the love of Abraham our father, peace
be upon him.*

III   The ten trials with which Abraham our father was
tried are all stated in Scripture. The first, that of being
a stranger, when the One to be blessed said,[6] ". . . betake yourself out of your country. . . ." The second,
the famine that existed in the land of Canaan when
he came there and He had promised him,[7] ". . . and I
will make you into a great nation. . . ." This is a great
trial, as it said,[8] "And there was a famine in the
land. . . ." The third, the wrong perpetrated upon him
by the Egyptians when Sarah was taken to Pharaoh.[9]
The fourth, his warring with the four kings.[10] The fifth,
his taking Hagar for a wife after he despaired of be-
getting through Sarah.[11] The sixth is circumcision, concerning which he was commanded in the period of old
age.[12] The seventh, the wrong perpetrated upon him by
the king of Gerar when he, too, took Sarah.[13] The

eighth, the banishment of Hagar after he had begotten a son through her.[14] The ninth, the removal of his son Ishmael, and the One to be blessed said,[15] ". . . let it not be grievous in your sight because of the lad . . . ," and Scripture had attested how difficult this matter was in his sight when it stated,[16] "And the matter was very grievous in Abraham's sight. . . ." However, he kept the commandment of the Lord, may He be blessed, and banished them.[17] The tenth, the binding of Isaac.[18]

> *IV   Ten wonders were wrought for our fathers in Egypt and ten at the sea. (Ten plagues did the Holy One, blessed be He, bring upon the Egyptians in Egypt and ten at the sea.) With ten trials did our fathers try the Omnipresent in the wilderness, as it is said, ". . . yet you have tried Me these ten times and have not hearkened to My voice" (Numbers 14:22).*

IV   However, the ten wonders which were wrought for our fathers in Egypt is their deliverance from the ten plagues. Since each and every plague was set apart against the Egyptians and not against Israel, these are undoubtedly wonders. The language of the Torah with regard to each and every plague [verifies] that the Holy One, blessed be He, brought them only upon the Egyptians, except the plague of vermin where it did not clearly indicate this.[19] However, it is known that Israel was not punished [with the vermin], but they were present among them yet did not distress them, thus the sages explained.[20] With regard to the rest of the plagues, however, the matter was made clear through them.

Concerning the [plague of] blood it said,[21] ". . . and the Egyptians were unable to drink water from the river . . . ," proof that the damage affected them alone. Concerning the frogs it said,[22] ". . . and they shall enter into your house and into your bed-chamber. . . ." Concerning the wild beasts it said,[23] "And I will set apart in that day the land of Goshen. . . ." Concerning the murrain it said,[24] ". . . but of the cattle of the children of Israel not one died." Concerning the boils it said,[25] ". . . for the boils were upon the magicians and upon all the Egyptians." Concerning the hail it said,[26] "Only in the land of Goshen, where the children of Israel were, was there no hail." Concerning the locusts it said,[27] "And the locusts went up over all the land of Egypt. . . ." Concerning the darkness it said,[28] ". . . but all the children of Israel had light in their dwellings." [29]

However, the ten wonders which took place at the sea are [related in the] tradition.[30] The first, the dividing of the waters following the plain meaning of the verse,[31] ". . . and the waters were divided." The second, after they were divided they were made domelike so that it became as the likeness of a roof, neither flat nor sloped. The path was as if it were a tube through the waters. The waters being to the right, to the left, and above, it is [as] the statement of Habakkuk,[32] "You pierced its separated headwaters for the sake of his tribes. . . ." The third, its ground was hardened and enclosed for them, as it was said,[33] ". . . they walked upon dry land . . . ," and on its bed there did not remain any mud or slime as with the rest of rivers. The fourth, the paths of the Egyptians were through sticking mud, as it was said,[34] ". . . the 'mud' of mighty waters." The fifth, they (i.e., the waters) were divided into many paths equal to the number of the tribes, as the appearance of a rounded bow following this form: , as it was said,[35] "To Him who divided the Red Sea into sections. . . ." The sixth, the waters were congealed and hardened as stones, with reference to this it said,[36] ". . . You shattered the heads of the sea-monsters on the waters," meaning to say, the waters were hardened so that they became as something upon which heads may be broken. The seventh, they were not congealed after the same fashion of congealment as the rest of congealed waters, meaning to say, into one piece, but they became many pieces, as if they were stones and were ranged one upon another, as it was said,[37] "You broke the sea in pieces by Your strength. . . ." The eighth, it (i.e., the dome) was congealed as a crystal or an onyx, meaning to say, transparent so that they could see one another while they passed through it, as it was said,[38] ". . . darkness of waters, thick clouds of the skies," meaning to say, the gathering of the waters was like the essence of the heavens in clearness—for it is transparent. The ninth, sweet waters dripped from it (i.e., the dome) and they drank them. The tenth, they were congealed while they were dripping after they took of them what they drank before they descended to the ground, as it was said,[39] ". . . the drops stood upright as a heap, [the deeps congealed in the heart of the sea,]" meaning to say, the dripping matter was congealed in the heart of the sea.

We also find in the tradition that plagues came upon the Egyptians at the sea that were more numerous than the plagues of Egypt.[40] However, they all were of those same ten kinds that descended in Egypt but were divided into many kinds at the sea. This was alluded to when it was said,[41] ". . . these are the gods that smote the Egyptians with all manner of plagues in the widerness," meaning to say, at the widerness of the Red Sea.

However, the ten trials with which our fathers tried the Omnipresent are all statements of Scripture. The first, at the Red Sea, when they said,[42] ". . . because there were no graves in Egypt. . . ." The second, at Marah, as it was said,[43] "And the people murmured against Moses, saying: 'What shall we drink?'" The third, at the wilderness of Sin when they requested the Manna, where they said,[44] ". . . would that we had died by the hand of the Lord [in the land of Egypt . . .]." The fourth, their rebelliousness in leaving the Manna until the morning, as it was said,[45] ". . . some of them left it until the morning. . . ." The fifth, their rebelliousness when they sought it on the Sabbath day, as it is said,[46] "And it came to pass on the seventh day some of the people went out to gather. . . ." The sixth, at Rephidim, also concerning water.[47] The seventh, at Horeb, with the making of the calf.[48] The eighth, at Taberah, when they were in doubt at that place—when it said, "murmurers," as it was said,[49] "And the people were as murmurers. . . ." The ninth, at the graves of lust when they requested the flesh, as it was said,[50] "And the mixed multitude that was among them took to lusting. . . ." The tenth, at the wilderness of Paran with the incident of the spies, and there it was said,[51] ". . . yet you have tried Me these ten times and have not hearkened to My voice."

> *V   Ten wonders were wrought for our fathers in the Temple. No woman miscarried because of the odor of the sacred flesh. The sacred flesh never became rancid. No fly was seen in the slaughterhouse. No pollution befell the High Priest on the Day of Atonement. The rains did not extinguish the fire of the woodpile, nor did the wind overcome the column of smoke. No ritual defect was found in the Omer, the Two Loaves, and the Shew Bread.[1] The worshippers stood close together but prostrated themselves with ample room. Never did a serpent or scorpion cause injury in Jerusalem. No man said to his fellow, "The place is too strait for me" (Isaiah 49:20) that I should lodge in Jerusalem.*

V   You are aware that the altar was in the center of the Azarah, and we shall explain this in its place.[52] It was exposed to the heavens. Nevertheless, the rains would not extinguish the fire of the woodpile, nor would the wind disperse the column of smoke that ascended from the offerings, for at the time of the offering the air was dry. In the Azarah, each one would stand alongside his fel-

1. *Leviticus 23:9–14,17; 24:5–9.*

low, and at the time of prostrating they would not press one against another because of the greatness of their awe and calmness in that place.

> *VI   Ten things were created on the eve of Sab-*
> *bath at twilight, and these are they: the mouth of*
> *the earth, the mouth of the well, the mouth of the*
> *donkey, the bow, the manna, the rod, the shamir,*
> *the letters, the writing, and the tablets. Some say*
> *also the evil spirits, the grave of Moses, and the ram*
> *of Abraham our father. Some say also the tongs*
> *made with tongs.*

VI   *Also the tongs made with tongs*—who made the first? [53] In the Eighth Chapter we mentioned to you that they (i.e., the sages) did not believe in the periodic change of the Divine Will.[54] Rather, [they believed] that at the beginning of the fashioning of the phenomena, He instituted into nature that through them there would be fashioned all that would be fashioned. Whether the phenomenon which would be fashioned would be frequent, namely, a natural phenomenon, or it would be an infrequent change, namely, a sign, they are all equal.[55] Therefore, they said that [at twilight] on the sixth day He instituted into the nature of the earth that Korah and his company would sink [into it], and concerning the well, that it would bring forth the water, and concerning the donkey, that it would speak, and similarly for the rest.[56]

The letters refer to the Torah which was written before Him, may He be blessed—as it said; and it was not made known how this was accomplished, as it was said,[57] ". . . and I will give you the tablets of stone . . . [which I have written]." *The writing* refers to the script that was upon the tablets, as it said,[58] ". . . and the writing was the writing of God engraved upon the tablets."

Perhaps you will say that since all the wonders were instituted into the nature of those phenomena after the six days of creation, why then did he single out these ten? Know that he did not single them out in order to say that there is no other sign which was instituted into the nature of the phenomena except these. However, [in singling out these signs] he said that only these [ten] were fashioned at twilight [on the sixth day], and that the rest of the wonders and signs were instituted into the nature of the phenomena through which they were fashioned at the time when they were first fashioned.[59] They stated by way of illustration: [60] that when the waters were parted on the second day, it was instituted into [its] nature that the Red Sea would be parted for Moses, and the Jordan for Joshua, similarly for Elijah, and similarly for Elisha.[61] When the sun was created on the fourth day, it was instituted into its nature that it would stand still at that certain time when Joshua would address it.[62] Similarly for the rest of the wonders, except for these ten which were instituted into the nature of those phenomena [on the eve of Sabbath] at twilight.

The shamir is a small insect that cuts huge stones as it passes over them, and with it Solomon constructed the Temple.[63] *The tongs* are the implement with which the smith grips the hot iron in order that he may fashion it into what he might fashion.

> *VII   Seven things pertain to the unfinished man and seven pertain to the wise man. The wise man does not speak before one who is greater than he in wisdom, or before one who is older, and he does not interrupt the words of his colleague, and he is not confused to reply. He questions according to the subject and replies according to rule. He speaks on the first thing first and on the last thing last. Concerning what he has not understood, he says, "I have not understood," and he acknowledges the truth. Their opposites pertain to the unfinished man.*

VII   I shall first define these attributes that are often repeated in the teachings of the sages, namely, "empty," "ignorant," "unfinished," "wise," and "saintly." "Empty" refers to a man who does not have either intellectual or moral virtues, meaning to say, neither wisdom nor ethics. He also does not have acquired knowledge.[64] It is as if he is devoid of the good and of the evil, and he is the one who is termed "the empty man" because of his likeness to a field in which nothing of any kind was sown, and it is what is termed "an uncultivated field," as was made clear in Zera'im.[65]

"Ignorant" refers to a man who has moral virtues but does not have intellectual virtues, meaning to say, he has proper conduct ("derech eretz"), however, he does not possess [knowledge of the] Torah. He is the one who is termed "the ignorant man," meaning to say that he is beneficial for the general welfare and for the communities of states, since he has moral virtues through which his society and himself are benefited, as we explained in the introduction to our treatise.[66]

"Unfinished" refers to a man who has intellectual virtues and moral virtues. They, however, are not perfected, nor do they follow in proper sequence. Rather, they contain disarray and confusion, and are intermingled with deficiency [toward the completed state]. Therefore, he is termed "the unfinished man" so as to liken him to a utensil that would be made by a craftsman which would have its implemental form but which would lack completion and improvement. As the knife and the sword when the smith makes their unfinished forms—and they have attained their forms before he would whett them, sharpen them, polish them, and engrave upon them what he customarily engraves and complete their improvements, preceding this they are what are termed "unfinished metal utensils," as was made clear in Kellim.[67] It (i.e., "golem—unfinished") is a Hebrew word, [as in] "Your eyes beheld my unformed substance ("golmi") . . . ," meaning to say, my substance before it attained its human form.[68] Inasmuch as he has not attained this form in its completion, they termed him "the unfinished man" because of his likeness to a substance that is in readiness to receive a different form through which it would become more complete.

"Wise" refers to the man who has attained both types of virtues to perfection as required. "Saintly" refers to the wise man when he increases in virtue, meaning to say, in the moral virtues, so that he will incline a bit toward an extreme, as we explained in the Fourth Chapter, and his deeds will exceed his wisdom.[69] Therefore, he is termed "ḥasid—the saintly man" because of his increase [beyond the mean]. For the exaggeration in a matter would be termed "ḥasid," whether that exaggeration would be in the good or in the evil.[70]

He stated here that the wise man has these seven virtues, and they are major principles. Consequently, one should concentrate on them, for through them the knowledge, the study, and the practice is possible.[71] Four of them are moral virtues, namely, that he *does not speak before one who is greater than he in wisdom*, . . . *and he does not interrupt the words of his colleague*, but he would wait until he will complete his words. Neither would he glorify himself in what he does not know, as it was said, *Concerning what he has not understood, he says, "I have not understood*,*"* nor would he be obdurate; rather, when he hears the truth, he will acknowledge it. Even in what it is possible for him to thrust aside, or to dispute, or to distort, he would not wish to do it; this is as it was said, *and he acknowledges the truth*.

Three of them are intellectual virtues. [The first:] Were a sophist to lead him astray by means of the art of sophistry, he would not be confused and remain in doubt concerning the truth. Rather, he would quickly sense the area of the error and will clarify it, as it was said, *and he is not confused to reply*. This, however, will come to pass with skillful comprehension and careful cogitation of the sophist's statement, so as to understand the difference between the words.

The second virtue: He would question what is necessary to question relative to that matter; he would neither request a mathematical demonstration in the science of physics, nor an argument from physics in the mathematical sciences, and matters of the like.[72] If he were the one who were questioned, he would also answer in accordance with the subject of the question. [That is,] if he would be questioned in subjects which by their nature require a proof, he will answer in accordance with the subject of the questioner with a proof. If he would be questioned in that which is beneath this (i.e., which does not require a proof), he will answer according to that which is his opinion and [according to] its (i.e., the subject's) nature. Moreover, he would not be asked for the material cause to which he will offer the formal cause, or be asked for the formal cause to which he will offer the material cause.[73] Rather, he will reply from the standpoint of the object [of the question], as it was said, *He questions according to the subject and replies according to rule*. This will come to pass only after extraordinary wisdom.

The third virtue: He would set his learning in order and will give precedence to what is proper to be given precedence, and he will postpone what is proper to postpone, for this course avails greatly in learning, as it was said, *He speaks on the first thing first and on the*

last thing last. All these are in the reverse with regard
to the unfinished man inasmuch as he is incomplete, as
we explained, and he has not attained this superior degree.[74]

> *VIII   Seven kinds of retribution come upon the
> world for seven chief transgressions. If some give
> tithes and some do not give tithes, famine through
> drought ensues, some go hungry while some have
> enough. If all decided not to give tithes, famine
> through tumult and drought ensues. If all decided
> not to set apart the dough offering, an all-consum-
> ing famine ensues.[1] Pestilence comes upon the
> world for crimes warranting the death penalties
> prescribed by the Torah that were not brought
> before a court of law, and for [transgressing the
> laws of] seventh year produce.[2] The sword comes
> upon the world because of the delaying of justice
> and because of the perversion of justice, and be-
> cause of those who teach the Torah at variance with
> the Halachah.*

VIII   *Famine through drought* means that the year will
be one of scant rainfall; it will rain in some places and in
some it will not rain, and where it will rain, its rainfall
will be scant. *Famine through tumult* means that men
will be engaged in wars, quarrels, and vicissitudes that
will befall them, so that the land will lie fallow and will
not be sown at the time of sowing due to the public's anx-
ious condition. *An all-consuming famine* means that it

1. *Numbers 15:20.*   2. *Leviticus 25:1–7; 26:9.*

will not rain at all and the rivers and brooks will dry up,
as it was said,[75] "And the heavens that are above you
shall be brass. . . ." *The delaying of justice* means post-
poning the decision and reflecting upon it for many days
in a matter that is clear.[76] *The perversion of justice* means
that he will judge incorrectly.

> IX *Dangerous beasts come upon the world be-*
> *cause of perjury and for profanation of the Name.*
> *Exile comes upon the world because of idolatry, in-*
> *cest, and bloodshed, and for [transgressing the laws*
> *of] release of the land.*[1] *At four periods pestilence*
> *increases: in the fourth year, in the seventh year,*
> *in the year after the seventh year, and at the con-*
> *clusion of the Festival [of Tabernacles] every year.*
> *In the fourth year because of the [non-observance*
> *of the] poor-tithe due in the third year. In the*
> *seventh year because of the [non-observance of*
> *the] poor-tithe due in the sixth year. In the year af-*
> *ter the seventh year because of [transgressing the*
> *laws of] seventh year produce. At the conclusion*
> *of the Festival [of Tabernacles] every year because*
> *of the robbing of the gifts prescribed to the poor.*

IX In numerous instances in the Order of Zera'im we
have explained the order of extracting the portions from
the produce. There it was made clear that in the third
and sixth years one would extract the first tithe and give
it to the Levite as in every year, then one would extract
the poor-tithe and give it to the poor. This poor-tithe

1. *Leviticus 25:3f; 26:4f. Deuteronomy 15:1.*

is in place of the second tithe which one would extract throughout the remaining years of the release (i.e., the seven-year cycle).[77]

Gifts prescribed to the poor are the stalks gleaned after the harvest, the forgotten sheaf, the corner of the field, the fallen fruit, and the gleanings of the vineyard.[78] [*Pestilence increases . . . At the conclusion of the Festival,*] for at the Festival all this will be consummated inasmuch as the work of the field was completed.[79] He who has given these portions has given them, and he who has not given them has robbed them.[80]

> X   *There are four characteristics among men:*
> *One who says, "What is mine is mine and what*
> *is yours is yours"—this is the median attribute,*
> *and some say this is the attribute of* [*the men of*]
> *Sodom. "What is mine is yours and what is yours is*
> *mine" is an ignorant man. "What is mine is yours*
> *and what is yours is yours" is a saintly man. "What*
> *is mine is mine and what is yours is mine" is a*
> *wicked man.*

X   Behold, through this statement it was made clear that the saintly man is one who will increase in the good deeds, meaning to say that he will incline a bit toward one of the two extremes.[81] It was also made clear to you that he who has of the vices of the soul would be termed "a wicked man," meaning to say that in his deeds he will incline toward the other extreme—the excess, as we explained in the Fourth Chapter.[82] For one who will desire to possess his own money and someone else's money has "excessive passion," and he termed him "a wicked man."

> *XI There are four characteristics among tempera-ments: Easy to provoke and easy to soothe—his gain is negated by his loss. Difficult to provoke and difficult to soothe—his loss is negated by his gain. Difficult to provoke and easy to soothe is a saintly man. Easy to provoke and difficult to soothe is a wicked man.*

XI Consider how he termed the forbearing man whose forbearance is inordinate until he will draw near to [the extreme of] insensibility with regard to the matter of anger—"a saintly man." [83] And he termed one who has the vice of anger "a wicked man."

> *XII There are four characteristics among students: Quick to understand and quick to lose—his gain is negated by his loss. Slow to understand and slow to lose—his loss is negated by his gain. Quick to un-derstand and slow to lose is a wise man. Slow to understand and quick to lose—this is an evil lot.*

XII Consider how he did not term the sagacious man who is endowed with a good memory "a saintly man," because this constitutes an intellectual virtue, and he termed him "a wise man." And he did not term the man who has difficulty in comprehending subjects and who is excessive in forgetfulness "a wicked man," because it is not within his power [to comprehend and to remember], and they are not of the virtues that are possible to acquire, as we explained in the Second Chapter.[84]

> *XIII   There are four characteristics among alms-givers: One who desires to give but that others should not give—his eye is evil towards that which belongs to others; that others should give but that he should not give—his eye is evil towards that which belongs to him; gives and [desires] that others should give is a saintly man; does not give and [desires] that others should not give is a wicked man.*

XIII   Consider how he termed the man who is excessive in mercy and who would not be content that he alone should be merciful until others too will be merciful—"a saintly man." And he termed the cruel man "a wicked man." [85]

> *XIV   There are four characteristics among those who go to the house of study: [One who] goes but does not practice has the recompense for going; practices but does not go has the recompense for practicing; goes and practices is a saintly man; neither goes nor practices is a wicked man.*

XIV   His statement . . . *among those who go to the house of study;* meaning thereby, concerning going to the house of study there are four characteristics. Consider how he termed one who increases in acquiring virtues "a saintly man," and one who is slothful in acquiring, "a wicked man." When you know the intellectual virtues and the moral virtues, and you know all their types, if you wish [you may refer to these as] the study of wisdom and the practice; and you know the middle course and the way of practice, which would be termed "good qualities" (i.e., virtues), and the slight increase beyond the middle course—that it is of the deeds of recognized saints; [86] and you know the [extreme of] excess and the [extreme of] deficiency —that both are reprehensible, except that one of the extremes is more properly designated with the appellation "evil," while the other would be termed "sin," or improper deed; and the illustration with regard to this: "moderation" undoubtedly is an absolute good (i.e., virtue), "excessive passion" undoubtedly is an absolute evil, and although "insensibility with regard to pleasure" is an evil, indeed it is not the same as "excessive passion" and it would be termed "sin," or improper deed —and the slight departure from "moderation" toward the side of "insensibility" is deemed proper for the perfect (i.e., the saintly); [87] and when you comprehend this subject, you will know that he who departed slightly from "moderation" would be termed "a saintly man," as we previously stated, and that one who is "insensible" would be termed "sinner." Therefore, it was said with regard to the Nazirite, ". . . in that he sinned against the soul," as we explained in the Fourth Chapter.[88]

From all that we previously stated and explained you will know who among men is worthy of being termed "empty," who is worthy of being termed "ignorant," who is worthy of being termed "unfinished," who is worthy of being termed "wise," who is worthy of being termed "wicked," who is worthy of being termed "saintly," and who is worthy of being termed "sinner." According to what we previously stated by way of The Commentary, these seven appellations apply to the seven [types of] men according to what they possess of the virtues and of the vices—the moral and the intellectual.[89]

They have applied appellations according to the qualities of the man. As in the instance where one has moral vices, and as we explained, he is the one who is termed "a wicked man," and if he were to have intellectual virtues which he would utilize for evil deeds, according to the sages, this type would be termed "guilefully wicked." If he were a wicked man who causes harm to people, meaning to say that included in the moral vices there would be qualities which will cause harm to people, such as brazenness, cruelty, and matters of the like, this type would be termed "evilly wicked." [90] Thus he who will possess intellectual virtues and moral vices with which he will cause harm would be termed "wise to do evil," as the verse stated with reference to him who is as such,[91] ". . . they are wise to do evil, but to do good they have no knowledge," meaning to say that they would utilize their intellectual virtues for evil deeds and not for good deeds.

Concerning the man in whom all the virtues will be combined, the intellectual and the moral virtues, so that there will not be either an intellectual virtue or a virtue of the moral virtues that is not in him, this type is rarely found. The philosophers state that the existence of such a man is very improbable but it is not impossible, and were he to be found, they would term him "the godlike man." [92] Thus in our language he would be termed "the man of God." [93] I, however, say that that man would be termed "a messenger of the Lord," as it said,[94] "And a messenger of the Lord came up from Gilgal. . . ." The philosophers stated that it is impossible that a man in whom were combined all the vices without exception would be found, devoid of the intellectual as well as the moral so that he would not have a virtue at all—and were he to be found, and it is improbable, they would figuratively designate him with the name of one of the dangerous beasts that inflicts harm.[95] Thus, Solomon termed him ". . . a bear robbed of his whelps . . . ," since he is a combination of folly and harm.[96]

These five are also compound appellations. Four express contempt—they are: "guilefully wicked," "evilly wicked," "wise to do evil," and "bear robbed of his whelps; one expresses greatness, and there is none greater than it, namely, "the man of God," or "a messenger of the Lord." Scripture has made clear that the term for the man in whom there will be found the intellectual virtues and the moral virtues is "a messenger of the Lord," as it was said,[97] ". . . the priest's lips shall keep knowledge and they shall seek the Torah at his mouth, for he is a messenger of the Lord of Hosts." "Knowledge" incorporates all the intellectual virtues inasmuch as one will become perfect only after they are attained.[98] It stated, ". . . they shall seek the Torah at his mouth . . . ," proof of his perfection in the moral virtues according to what we explained in the Fourth Chapter.[99] For this is the purpose of the Torah, therefore, it said,[100] ". . . and all her paths are peace," and we have also explained there that "peace" constitutes the moral virtues.[101] Subsequently, it stated, ". . . for he is a messenger of the Lord of Hosts."

> *XV   There are four characteristics among those who sit before the sages: the sponge, the funnel, the strainer, and the sieve. The sponge, for it absorbs everything. The funnel, for it takes in at one end and lets out at the other. The strainer, for it lets out the wine and keeps the lees. The sieve, for it lets out the [thin] flour and keeps the [thick] fine flour.*

XV   He likened the man who is endowed with a good memory and who will remember everything he hears but would not distinguish between the true and the false—to the sponge, and it is wool of the sea which soaks up everything. He also likened one who will comprehend immediately but would not remember anything at all, neither the genuine nor the spurious—to the funnel. He likened one who will remember the incorrect matters and the spurious knowledge but would forget the genuine matters upon which practice is based—to the strainer, for only the lees would remain in it and it will let out the pure. He likened the man in whom the case is the opposite—to the sieve, for it lets out the dust and the grit through its holes and the fine flour would remain in it. This refers only to the flour sieve, it is the best among them since it lets out the thin flour which has no use, and it retains the thick, namely, the fine flour.

> XVI All friendship that is dependent on a [material] thing, when the thing ceases the friendship ceases. That which is not dependent on a thing will never cease. Which friendship depended on a thing? This was the friendship of Amnon and Tamar.¹ Which did not depend on a thing? This was the friendship of David and Jonathan.²

XVI The explanation of these words is as thus.¹⁰² You are aware that these sensual motives will cease and depart, and the departure of what was brought into being will be necessitated by the departure of its motive. Consequently, when the motive of the friendship will be a metaphysical subject, and it is the genuine knowledge, it is impossible for that friendship to ever depart, because its motive exists eternally.¹⁰³

> XVII Every controversy that is for the sake of Heaven will end in enduring value. That which is not for the sake of Heaven will not end in enduring value. Which controversy was for the sake of Heaven? This was the controversy of Hillel and

1. I Samuel 13:1f.   2. I Samuel 18:1; II Samuel 1:26.

Shammai. Which was not for the sake of Heaven?
This was the controversy of Korah and all his
company.

XVII   All this is clear. These subjects [as related in
this Mishnah and the next] are [taught] from the standpoint of reward and punishment. For he who will dispute not for the purpose of contradicting his fellow's
words but because of his desire to know the truth, his
words will endure and will not be cut off.

XVIII   Whoever causes the many to be virtuous,
no sin will ensue because of him. Whoever causes
the many to sin will not be given the opportunity
to repent. Moses was virtuous and made the many
virtuous, and the virtue of the many is ascribed to
him, as it is said, ". . . he executed the righteousness
of the Lord and His judgments with Israel" (Deu-
teronomy 33:21). Jeroboam sinned and caused the
many to sin, and the sin of the many is ascribed to
him, as it is said, ". . . because of the sin of Jero-
boam, which he sinned and wherewith he caused
Israel to sin" (I Kings 14:16).

XVIII   Everyone who will direct people aright, the
Lord, may He be blessed, will reward him by precluding him from sin. Whereas everyone who will lead people
astray, the Lord, may He be blessed, will punish him
by precluding him from repentance. This is clear and

there is no difficulty in it when you comprehend what we incorporated in the Eighth Chapter.[104]

> *XIX   Everyone who possesses these three traits is of the disciples of Abraham our father, [everyone who possesses] three other traits is of the disciples of Balaam the wicked—a good eye, a lowly spirit, and a humble soul is of the disciples of Abraham our father; an evil eye, a lofty spirit, and an insatiable soul is of the disciples of Balaam the wicked. What is the difference between the disciples of Abraham our father and the disciples of Balaam the wicked? The disciples of Abraham our father are sustained in this world and inherit The World To Come, as it is said, "That I may cause them that love Me to inherit substance and that I may fill their treasure-houses" (Proverbs 8:21). However, the disciples of Balaam the wicked inherit Gehinnom and descend to the pit of destruction, as it is said, "Thou God will bring them down to the pit of destruction, men of blood and deceit shall not live out half their days, but I will trust in Thee" (Psalms 55:24).*

XIX   *A good eye. . . .* In numerous instances we have explained that the meaning of *a good eye* is "contentedness," *a humble soul* is "moderation," and *a lowly spirit* is "inordinate modesty," as was made clear in the preceding chapter.[105] The three that are over against them are: "lust for acquiring money" is *an evil eye,* "excessive passion" is *an insatiable soul,* and "pride" is a *lofty spirit.* Those three virtues were widely known as belonging to Abraham our father; accordingly, everyone in whom these three virtues shall be found would be termed . . . *of the disciples of Abraham our father,* inasmuch as he conducted himself with his attributes. Whereas everyone in whom these three vices shall be found is . . . *of the disciples of Balaam the wicked,* since he conducted himself with his attributes.

I shall now note the places where through them it was made clear that all these virtues pertain to Abraham and all those vices pertain to Balaam, and they are all found in the Torah. Concerning "contentedness" with regard to Abraham—he said to the king of Sodom,[106] "That I will not take a thread or a shoe-latchet nor anything that is yours . . . ," and this is the ultimate of contentedness—where a man will forsake a great sum of money and will not derive benefit from it even in a trifling matter. Concerning his "moderation"—he said to Sarah on the day of his coming to Egypt, ". . . behold now I know that you are a fair woman to look upon," and through the interpretation it was mentioned that he had not totally looked at her form save on that day—this is the ultimate of moderation.[107] Moreover, he said [to Sarah] with reference to Hagar after he had taken her [as his concubine],[108] ". . . behold your maid is in your hand, do to her that which is good in your sight," which denotes that he had no desire to derive enjoyment from her. Thus, when Sarah requested him to banish her with Ishmael in order that she preclude him from turning to her for sexual relations, Scripture attested that this was grievous in his sight only as it pertained to Ishmael, as it was said,[109] "And the matter was very grievous in Abraham's sight on account of his son." All these are signs of "moderation." Concerning his "modesty"—he said,[110] ". . . and I am dust and ashes."

"Lust for money" was widely known as belonging to Balaam the wicked, namely, his coming from Aram Naharaim for the sake of the money with which he was hired to curse Israel, as the One to be blessed stated,[111] ". . . and they hired against you Balaam the son of Beor [from Pethor of Aram Naharaim to curse you]." Indeed, his "excessive passion" with regard to the subject of sexual relations is the motive of his advice to Balak, [namely,] that he declare the women [of Moab] free to play the harlot with Israel, and that he establish publicly recognized prostitutes. For were it not for the excessive passion which he had, and since harlotry was a good thing in his sight, he would not have counselled it, for men's counsel is nothing other than that which is in accord with their opinion. Good men will not counsel evil; instead, they will caution against it. The language of Scripture [verifies that this indeed was counselled by Balaam, in saying],[112] "Behold these women of Moab caused the children of Israel through the counsel of Balaam. . . ." And the sages said: [113] Balaam was a sodomist—and there is no doubt concerning it, because he whose opinion is such, such will be his deed. Concerning his "pride"—he said,[114] "The saying of him who hears the word of God. . . ." However, they adduced proof concerning Balaam from the statement, "*Thou God will bring them down to the pit of destruction, men of blood [and deceit shall not live out half their days . . .],*" meaning, that he was a man of blood inasmuch as he was the cause of the death of [tens of thousands of the children of] Israel through the plague, and he was also a man of deceit when he fashioned stratagems for evil deeds.[115] They adduced proof concerning the disciples of Abraham from the statement, "*That I may cause them that love Me to inherit substance and that I may fill their treasurehouses,*" just as Scripture termed him (i.e., the disciple of Abraham) ". . . the seed of Abraham My beloved." [116]

> XX   *Judah ben Tema said: Be bold as a leopard, fleet as an eagle, swift as a gazelle, and courageous as a lion to do the will of your Father who is in Heaven. He used to say: The boldfaced man is for Gehinnom, and the shamefaced man for the Garden of Eden. May it be Your will, Lord our God, that Your city be rebuilt speedily in our days, and grant that our portion be in Your Torah.*

XX   Although he said, *The boldfaced man is for Gehinnom*, he counselled boldness in rebuking the rebellious, and in matters of the like. It is as if he said, make use of some of the vices in their place, [that is,] for the will of the Lord, may He be blessed, and for His truth, as the statement of the prophet,[117] ". . . and with the crooked You are subtle." [However, you may do this] only upon the condition that your intention will be the truth, as it was said, *to do the will of your Father who is in Heaven.*

Of the good qualities that the Lord, may He be blessed, vouchsafed to this nation—that they have shame-facedness. Thus they said: [118] The signs of the seed of Abraham are that they are meek, merciful, and kind; and it said, ". . . that the fear of Him be upon your faces so that you do not sin." After as he described the virtues of shamefacedness, he supplicated and said, "Lord our God, as You have vouchsafed to us this virtue, so shall You vouchsafe to us to rebuild Your city speedily in our days."

> *XXI   He used to say: At five years of age [one is ready] for the Bible, at ten years for the Mishnah, at thirteen years for the precepts, at fifteen years for the Gemara, at eighteen years for marriage, at twenty years for pursuing [a worldly occupation], at thirty years for strength, at forty years for understanding, at fifty years for counsel, at sixty years for old age, at seventy years for gray hairs, at eighty years for might, at ninety years for bowing [under the weight of many decades], at one hundred years one is as though he were dead and had passed away and ceased from the world.*

> *XXII   Ben Bag Bag said: Turn it and turn it for everything is in it, and by means of it you will perceive. Grow gray and old in it and do not stir from it, for you cannot have a more excellent rule than it.*

XXII   With regard to the Torah he said that one should turn it and meditate in it because everything is in it.[119] And he said, . . . *and by means of it you will perceive* ("teh'ḥehzey"), meaning to say, [you will perceive] the truth; meaning, you will behold ("v'thireh") the truth through the inner eye of the intellect—as the Targum translation of "va'yar—and he beheld," is "va'ḥaza—and he perceived." [120] Subsequently, he said, *Grow gray and old in it . . .* , that is to say, engage in it until the time of old age, and even then do not depart from it to something else.

> *XXIII   Ben He He said: According to the suffering is the reward.*

XXIII   And Ben He He said, your recompense shall be according to what you will suffer in the [study of the] Torah.[121] They said: The only segment of wisdom that will endure is what you will learn through travail, toil, and awe of the teacher. However, studying for enjoyment and pleasure has no durability nor is their benefit in it. They said through interpretation of his statement,[122] ". . . also ("af") my wisdom remained with me," the wisdom that I learned through [the] wrath ("b'af") [of my teacher] remained with me. Therefore, he counselled to cast solemnity upon the students, and they said: [123] Project awe into the students.

1. Both the written and the oral traditions were received by Moses at Sinai. "Torah sheh'b'kthav," the written tradition, encompasses all the books of the Bible. "Torah sheh'b'alpeh," the oral tradition, represents all the enactments, decrees, and decisions that were rendered by the recipients of the written tradition. Thus, Rabbinic interpretations of Biblical statements have the effect of having been given to Moses at Sinai. The authoritative judge, or interpreter, is likened to a link in the chain of tradition. His decisions are to be followed because they represent what was transmitted to Moses. Introduction to The Commentary to The Mishnah, Wilna edition, fol. Berachoth, p. 108.

Maimonides' first publication of *The Commentary to The Mishnah* appeared in Egypt in 1168, see end of *The Commentary to The Mishnah*, hereafter called "The Commentary," at Uktzin, fol. Niddah, p. 77a. For the explanation of the discrepancy between Maimonides having been thirty years of age at its completion, i.e., in Morocco, 1165, or thirty-three years of age, i.e., in Egypt, 1168, see Baron, Salo W., *A Social and Religious History of The Jews*, Second Edition, N.Y., 1952, hereafter called "S. and R.," Vol. VI, p. 351, n. 65.

2. Leviticus 18:30.

3. Yebamoth 21a.

4. One does not serve God nor fulfill His precepts for the purpose of receiving a reward. This was perceived by Antigonus of Socho. The person who serves God out of love is he who believes in the truth for the sake of the truth. The Commentary, Sanhedrin 10:1, p. 246.

5. Deuteronomy 6:13.

6. Palestinian Talmud, Berachoth 9:7 (Krotoschin edition), p. 142. "And they said" refers to a well-known saying that is found in Arabic moralistic literature. See Kapaḥ, Joseph, *Mishnah im Perush Rabbenu Mosheh ben Maimon*, Mossad Harav Kook, Israel, 1964, hereafter called "Kapaḥ," p. 268, n. 13.

7. For negative precepts and positive precepts, see infra, Ch. II, n. 4. Precepts whose rationale rests on revelation alone are explained by Maimonides as follows: One is commanded to curb one's desires. However, one may not say that by nature he does not wish to transgress one of the precepts that teaches this. For example, one should not say, ". . . I do not want to wear garments made of a mixture of wool and linen" (Leviticus 19:19). Rather, he should say, "I do desire to, yet I must not, for my Father in Heaven has forbidden it." See Gorfinkle, J. I., *The Eight Chapters of Maimonides on Ethics*, N.Y., 1912, hereafter called "Eight Chapters," Ch. VI, pp. 76–8.

8. That is, of the righteous being rewarded and the wicked being punished. The eleventh of the Thirteen Divine Attributes is that God will reward the righteous with the life of The World To Come, and will punish the wicked with Extirpation, i.e., its forfeiture. The Commentary, Sanhedrin 10:1, pp. 247–8. Cp. infra, Ch. II, ns. 63, 7.

9. The community, namely, the accepted view of the sages.

10. The "fundamental principle" being the existence of God. To deny it is to be of the opinion that neither the written nor the oral tradition was Divinely revealed, and that God will not reward the righteous and punish the wicked. Only some people believed that the written Torah was genuine and that the oral tradition was spurious. Zadok and Boethus denied the validity of both. They, however, feigned belief in the written Torah.

11. Maimonides' discussion of the origins of the Saducees and Boethusians is based on the passage in *Aboth De Rabbi Nathan*, Schechter, S., ed., N.Y., 1945, hereafter called "ARN," Rec. A, Ch. 5, p. 26. On the origins of the Saducees and Boethusians, see Finkelstein, Louis, *The Pharisees*, Third Edition, Phila., 1962, Vol. II, pp. 762–779. Maimonides' definition of heterodoxical Karaism of his day as an expression of Saduceeanism cannot be considered historical. His view is understandable insofar as the cardinal point of Karaism centered about its rejec-

tion of the oral tradition. For a history of the origins of Karaism ca. 767 C.E. stemming from an interaction of the political and social actualities of the Moslem world and the politics of the Jewish community of Persia-Babylon, see S. and R., Vol. V, p. 210f.

12. Deuteronomy 17:11.

13. For the significance of names presented in pairs, see infra, Ch. IV, n. 113.

14. Abraham was noted for his hospitality to wayfarers. Genesis Rabbah 54:8 (Warsaw edition), Vol. I, p. 642; ARN, Rec. A, Ch. 7, pp. 33-4.

15. Kapaḥ renders this sentence as follows: Thus the sages rejected purchasing slaves and preferred to use the services of the poor because they are one's kith and kin, see p. 269. Apparently, Maimonides counsels the hiring of a poor Israelite rather than the purchase of a slave. This practice would be consistent with the highest of his eight degrees of charity, namely, to aid the poor in such manner that they may support themselves, see *Mishneh Torah*, hereafter called "M.T.," Hilchoth Mattenoth Anniyim 10:7-13. Cp. "If your brother wax poor and his means fail . . . you shall uphold him . . . ," Leviticus 25:35.

16. For Maimonides' application of the teachings of Aristotle to Jewish ethics, see Eight Chapters, Ch. IV, p. 54, n. 1. Virtue represents the mean between the opposite extremes of excess and deficiency. An action practiced in either extreme is considered a vice. In his actions, the wise man observes the middle course. The saintly man does not practice the precise mean; as a precautionary measure calculated to counterbalance a possible tendency toward an extreme, he inclines his action somewhat toward its opposite extreme, infra, Ch. IV, pp. 65-6; Ch. V, pp. 110-11.

17. "Gehinnom," the abode of the wicked who fail to merit the life of The World To Come. From "Geh ben Hinnom— the valley of the son of Hinnom," the Moloch infanticide ritual was practiced there, Jeremiah 7:31-2.

18. The precise source is unknown. However, we may offer these statements as parallels: A man who studies on his own cannot be on a par with a man who learns from his master,

Kethuboth 111a. Just as fire cannot burn by itself, thus the words of the Torah cannot endure when one studies on his own. . . . Just as the small piece of wood kindles the large, thus lesser scholars sharpen the greater, Ta'anith 7a.

19. Ta'anith 23a.

20. ". . . for his friend is another self . . . ," *Nicomachean Ethics,* in *Great Books of the Western World,* Hutchins, R. M., ed., Chicago, 1952, hereafter called "G.B.," Vol. IX, Book IX, Ch. IV, p. 419.

21. "Perfect friendship is the friendship of men who are good, and alike in virtue; for these wish well alike to each other qua good, and they are good in themselves." Aristotle's discussion of the three types of friendship, ibid., Book VIII, Ch. III, pp. 407–8.

22. Sabbath 97a.

23. Proverbs 26:25.

24. Although an action is inclined toward an extreme, in terms relative to counterbalancing a tendency toward its opposite extreme, it is to be considered a virtue. For example: a) Lavishness is the extreme of excess, generosity is the virtue, parsimony is the extreme of deficiency; the saintly man would incline somewhat toward the extreme of lavishness, Eight Chapters, Ch. IV, pp. 60–1. b) Anger is the extreme of excess, forbearance is the virtue, insensibility to disgrace is the extreme of deficiency; the saintly man would incline somewhat toward the extreme of insensibility to disgrace, infra, Ch. V, pp. 108–9, and n. 83.

25. Man is not created with innate moral virtues or vices; they are acquired environmentally, Eight Chapters, Ch. IV, p. 58.

26. Idleness leads to lewdness, Kethuboth 59b.

27. Sanhedrin 103b.

28. The words "in former times" are deleted, Kapaḥ, p. 271; cp. infra, Ch. II, p. 31, and n. 28. Doeg, see I Samuel 22:9–23.

29. "Apikorsuth—heresy." The term "Apikoros—heretic" is derived from the Greek "Ἐπικύρος." For Maimonides' use of the term, see infra, Ch. II, pp. 42–3, and n. 62. Instead of "from them," Kapaḥ reads "from you," p. 271. Zadok and Boethus

concluded that ". . . man has neither reward nor punishment, and there is no expectation at all," supra, p. 4.

30. ARN, Rec. A, Ch. 12, p. 48f.

31. Malachi 2:6.

32. "Yasef—will be consumed," as in ". . . will You consume ("tispeh") the righteous with the wicked," Genesis 18:23. "K'tala—execution," with reference to the case of one who gathered sticks on the Sabbath (Numbers 15:32–6), according to the Talmud he was a "bar k'tala—one who deserves execution." However, Moses was unaware of the mode of execution to be applied, Sanhedrin 78b; cp. infra, Ch. II, n. 6.

33. Infra, Ch. IV, p. 71f.

34. Kapah reads, "That is to say, it is forbidden for him to render service to a sage except if he is a disciple of his," p. 271.

35. The text reads "Second Chapter." If action could be determined by an external force, then there is no freedom of choice, Eight Chapters, Ch. VIII, pp. 87–8.

36. Proverbs 22:6. The authorship of Proverbs is attributed to Solomon, Proverbs 1:1.

37. For Maimonides' attitudes regarding the pursuit of scholarship and worldly occupation, see Baron, S. W., "The Economic Views of Maimonides," in *Essays on Maimonides*, Baron, S. W., ed., N.Y., 1941, p. 146.

38. Baba Metzia 87a.

39. Genesis 18:5–8.

40. Ephron's words were very considerate. He spoke of "giving" Abraham the burial ground. However, he exacted an exorbitant price for it, ibid., 23:11–17.

41. Mishnah VI and The Commentary, supra, p. 7.

42. Palestinian Talmud, Mo'ed Katan 1:10, p. 81a.

43. The three types of tithes, infra, Ch. V, pp. 107–8.

44. Proverbs 10:19.

45. Ecclesiastes 5:2.

46. Kiddushin 71b.

47. Source unknown.

48. Deuteronomy 6:7. ". . . and the study of Torah is the equivalent of them all," M. Peah 1:1.

49. *The Mishneh Torah* contains an entire section devoted to

this subject. "Hilchoth Talmud Torah—Laws regarding the study of Torah," consists of seven chapters containing eighty-two paragraphs.

50. Leviticus 19:11, 14, 16.

51. "It was said of Rav, the disciple of Rabbenu HaKaddosh," M.T., Hilchoth De'oth 2:4.

52. Tosefta Yebamoth 8:4 (Zuckermandel, M.S., ed.), p. 250.

53. Baba Bathra 75a.

54. Psalms 33:1.

55. Pesaḥim 3b.

56. Various precepts of the Torah are intended to incline man toward one extreme so as to remove him from its opposite extreme, Eight Chapters, Ch. IV, pp. 65–6.

57. Tosefta Sanhedrin 12:10, p. 433.

58. Baba Bathra 164b.

59. Arachin 15b.

60. Sabbath 56b.

61. Proverbs 26:18–19.

62. The incident of Rabbi Simeon, the son and student of Rabbi Judah HaNasi, Baba Bathra 164b. If "Dust of slander" could elicit so strong a rebuke as "Betake yourself from slander," how much more does it imply to flee from slander itself! Thus, the maximum removal from slander is to be clear of the dust of slander.

63. M. Arachin 3:5.

64. Numbers 13:12.

65. Arachin 15a.

66. Not found in the Tosefta. The Palestinian Talmud, however, reads, "For four things man receives retribution in this world and the stock of which remains for him in The World To Come, and these are they: idolatry, incest, and bloodshed—and slander is the equivalent of them all," Peah 1:1, p. 15b.

67. Arachin 15b.

68. Exodus 32:31.

69. Genesis 39:9.

70. Ibid., 4:13.

71. Arachin 15b with reference to Psalms 12:4.

72. Arachin 15b with reference to Psalms 12:5. The funda-

mental principle, supra, n. 10. Instead of "this sin which arouses" ("ha'm'orer"), Kapaḥ reads, "this accursed sin" ("ha'arur"), p. 275.

73. Eight Chapters, Ch. IV, p. 64.

1. Eight Chapters, Ch. IV, pp. 54-5.

2. Rejoicing on the festival, Deuteronomy 16:14. Teaching the sacred language, ibid., 6:7.

3. Circumcision, Genesis 17:10. Fringes, Numbers 15:38. Paschal sacrifice, Exodus 12:6.

4. The total number of Biblical precepts is 613; 248 are positive precepts and 365 are negative precepts. For an enumeration of the precepts and a listing of their Biblical sources, see Blackman, P., *Mishnayoth*, Second Edition, N.Y., 1964, Vol. VII, pp. 67-88.

5. Transgressions which entail no concrete action and for which the punishment of Stripes is not levied, such as, ". . . that you bring not blood upon your house . . ." Deuteronomy 22:8. Cp. infra, n. 20.

6. Stoning, Burning, Sword, and Strangulation. In relatively few instances is the mode of execution Biblically prescribed. In cases involving the death penalty and where the mode is not Biblically prescribed, Rabbinic jurisprudence derives it by means of "Gezerah Shavah," the comparing of similar, or analogous verses in two or more Biblical passages. See "Capital Punishment," in *The Jewish Encyclopedia*, N.Y., 1912, Vol. III, pp. 544-8.

7. Forfeiture of the life of The World To Come, Sanhedrin 64b; M.T., Hilchoth T'shubah 8:1. Maimonides' interpretation of The World To Come, infra, n. 63.

8. Maximum of forty stripes less one, Deuteronomy 25:3; Makkoth 22b. Maimonides rules that all transgressions of negative precepts that incur the punishment of Extirpation and not one of the four modes of Execution, are punishable by

Stripes. So too, all transgressions of negative precepts that incur the punishment of Death by an Act of Heaven, or transgressions of negative precepts which involve the commission of a specific action, such as transgressing the proscription of wearing garments of forbidden mixtures (Deuteronomy 22:11), are punishable by Stripes, M.T., Hilchoth Sanhedrin 18:1.

9. Supra, n. 5.

10. Sukkah 25a.

11. Yoma 33a.

12. Supra, n. 3.

13. Exodus 23:12.

14. Deuteronomy 22:8.

15. Not to perform work on the Sabbath, Exodus 20:10. The punishment for performing work on the Sabbath is Stoning, Numbers 15:32–6.

16. The precept to perform circumcision refers to two instances: a) a father is required to circumcise his son at the age of eight days, supra, n. 3; b) the uncircumcised adult is required to circumcise himself, Genesis 17:14. The punishment for neglecting to perform circumcision in either instance is Extirpation, see Maimonides' *Sefer HaMitzvoth*, Positive Precept no. 215.

17. Numbers 28:2.

18. Supra, n. 7.

19. Supra, n. 5.

20. Deuteronomy 22:8. Two separate precepts, a positive and a negative, are found in this one verse. However, the negative precept, ". . . that you bring not blood upon your house. . . ," follows in explication of the positive precept, ". . . you shall make a parapet. . . ." Where this type of negative precept obtains, i.e., as a result of the omission to perform the positive precept, the punishment of Stripes is not prescribed, Pesaḥim 95a.

21. The concluding part of the syllogism is derived from the inference drawn in n. 20. Since the punishment of Stripes is not incurred for transgressing the negative precept, ". . . that you bring not blood upon your house. . . ," the performance of the positive precept, ". . . you shall make a parapet. . . ," bears a relatively lesser recompense.

22. In his discussion of freedom of choice as opposed to pre-determination, Maimonides reasons that reward and punishment cannot exist if there were no freedom of choice. In order to demonstrate this he cites the precept, ". . . you shall make a parapet. . . ," to indicate that, if everything were predetermined, why then this prescription and others like it? Eight Chapters, Ch. VIII, pp. 87–8.

23. Kiddushin 39b.

24. Prior to his publication of The Commentary, Maimonides completed a commentary to the Babylonian Talmud on the orders of Mo'ed, Nashim, Nezikin, and tractate Ḥullin of the order of Kodashim, see the Introduction to The Commentary, fol. Berachoth, p. 110; these are non-extant. However, in The Commentary, Maimonides notes that this refers to one who refrains from transgressing merely because of a Torahitic proscription, and that he is rewarded for desisting, see Makkoth 3:15, fol. Sanhedrin, p. 53.

25. Exodus 32:32. The nature of God's omniscience is beyond man's ability to comprehend, Eight Chapters, Ch. VIII, pp. 101–2. The tenth of the Thirteen Divine Attributes is that God is omniscient, The Commentary, Sanhedrin 10:1, p. 247.

26. Supra, Ch. I, p. 11.

27. He who does not teach his son a trade is as if he taught him to rob, Kiddushin 29a.

28. The words "in former times" are deleted, Kapaḥ, p. 276; cp. supra, Ch. I, p. 12. These words may have been added in order to shield Maimonides from possible disparagement regarding his close association with the government of Egypt. Keeping in mind Maimonides' outspoken opposition to the practice of accepting compensation for knowledge of the Torah (infra, Ch. IV, p. 71f), there is little doubt that in 1171 he accepted a position as a court physician under the patronage of the Vizir al-Fadil for the purpose of earning a livelihood, see Meyerhoff, M., "The Medical Works of Maimonides," in *Essays on Maimonides*, Baron, S. W., ed., N.Y., 1941, p. 268. Significantly, he was able to utilize his contact with the government to the advantage of the Jewish community. In 1175, Maimonides was instrumental in bringing about the deposal of

the infamous Nagid Zutta, see Neubauer, A., "Egyptian Frag-
ments," in *The Jewish Quarterly Review* (O.S.) Vol. VIII,
pp. 546–7. Moses Nahmanides mentions the assistance rendered
by Maimonides in behalf of the community of Yemen. He ef-
fected the nullification of various encumbering decrees and a
lightening of their tax burden, see *Kobetz T'shuboth Ha-
Rambam*, Lichtenberg, A. L., ed., Leipzig, 1859, Part III, 8d–
9a.

29. Infra, n. 54.

30. Supra, Ch. I, Mishnah XV.

31. Maimonides distinguishes between shamefacedness and diffidence. Shamefacedness represents the middle course between
boldness—the extreme of excess, and diffidence—the extreme of
deficiency, Eight Chapters, Ch. IV, pp. 56–7.

32. Genesis 32:25, Targum, ad loc.

33. Erubin 55a.

34. Deuteronomy 30:12–13. "The haughty," literally, "Those
of inflated spirit," an allusion to "It is not in heaven . . . who
will ascend. . . ." "Nor is it beyond the sea . . ." refers to
those who make extended trips.

35. Proverbs 5:22.

36. Psalms 7:16.

37. Sotah 8b.

38. Job 34:11.

39. The description of the powers of the Rational Faculty,
infra, n. 44, par. 5.

40. Deuteronomy 32:4.

41. Nehemiah 9:33.

42. Lamentations 3:36.

43. Everything from the conclusion of this paragraph through
the sentence in the preceding paragraph beginning with the
words, "But the righteous is gracious . . . ," is to be deleted,
Kapah, p. 278, n. 32.

44. The faculties of the soul are: the Nutritive, or the Growing, the Sensitive, the Imaginative, the Appetitive, and the Rational. Each faculty has its particular functions:

1) The Nutritive Faculty: a) Attraction of nourishment to
the body, b) Retention, c) Digestion, d) Repulsion of excess,

e) Growth, f) Procreation, g) Separation of nutritive fluids into those that are to be retained and those that are to be eliminated.

2) The Sensitive Faculty: a) Seeing, b) Hearing, c) Tasting, d) Smelling, e) Touching.

3) The Imaginative Faculty utilizes retained impressions perceived through the senses in different combinations resulting in ideas which were never perceived through the senses.

4) The Appetitive Faculty has among its psychic functions the power of desiring or abhorring, fear or courage, love or hate. The parts of the body and their respective functions are controlled by it: the hand to grasp, the heart to be courageous or timorous.

5) The Rational Faculty affords man the power of understanding, reflection, mastery of scientific knowledge, and differentiation between objectionable and acceptable actions. Its functions are subdivided into the Speculative and the Practical. Speculative power enables man to comprehend the sciences and to know things as they are in their essential and unchanging nature. Practical power is either Mechanical or Intellectual: the former enables the acquisition of such arts as architecture, medicine, and navigation; the latter affords man the ability to speculate on the implications of an action he conceived, consider the possibility of executing it, and if he considers it possible, to decide on the manner in which it should be performed. Eight Chapters, Ch. I, pp. 40–4.

The Moral Virtues are subsumed under the Appetitive Faculty. Among them are: Generosity, Uprightness, Contentedness, and Courage, ibid., Ch. II, p. 50. Cp. *On The Soul*, G.B., Vol. VIII, Book II, Chs. III-IV, pp. 644–8; Book III, Ch. XII, pp. 667–8.

45. Supra, n. 1.

46. Eight, Chapters, Ch. I, pp. 39–40.

47. Sabbath 105b.

48. Psalms 81:10.

49. Ibid., 58:5–6.

50. II Kings 5:20–7.

51. In rebuking Geḥazi, Elisha said, "Na'aman's leprosy shall cleave to you and to your seed forever . . ." (II Kings 5:27).

Concerning the words, ". . . to you and to your seed. . . ," the Talmud explains the verse, "And there were four leprous men at the entrance of the gate . . ." (II Kings 7:3) as referring to Gehazi and his three sons. Sanhedrin 107b.

52. Our edition of the Talmud reads: Our sages taught, always let the left hand repel and the right hand draw near, not as was done by Elisha who repelled Gehazi with both hands, Sanhedrin, loc. cit. That is, the rebuke was total and admitted no possibility of reconciliation. Interestingly, the passage should read as follows: Our sages taught, always let the left hand repel and the right hand draw near, not as was done by Elisha, who repelled Gehazi with both hands, and not as Rabbi Joshua ben Perahiah, who repelled Jesus with both hands, see Strack, Hermann, *Jesus die Heretiker und die Kristen*, Leipzig, 1910, pp. 10–11 (I am indebted to Professor Boaz Cohen for having made me aware of this information). Maimonides enjoyed the advantage of consulting a manuscript of the Babylonian Talmud that he believed to be about five hundred years old, see S. and R., Vol. VI, p. 21. In all likelihood, his edition of the Talmud had the complete text which cited both Gehazi and Jesus as examples of those who incurred the total rebuke of an offended master. Kapah reads, "You may know this from what happened to Gehazi with his master and to Jesus the Nazarene with his master Joshua ben Perahiah," p. 279.

53. Instead of "what his eyes behold," Kapah reads, ". . . the sight of his own species. . . ," p. 280.

54. To dispel melancholia Maimonides recommends listening to singing and music, viewing fine buildings, and art appreciation, Eight Chapters, Ch. V, p. 70. "Separateness" referred to here, in contradistinction to "separateness" from defilement (infra, Ch. III, p. 55, and n. 34), represents an act of virtue embarked upon by saintly men as a counterbalance to the deleterious effects of unavoidable contact with unwholesome deeds and attitudes. Saintly men would expurgate these influences through solitude and withdrawal, ibid., Ch. IV, p. 62; cf. supra, pp. 31–2.

55. Although a person may have a natural inclination toward either a moral or an intellectual virtue, he will not attain it unless he cultivates it. If he has a predilection towards a moral

virtue, he will find it easier to acquire; if he lacks the natural inclination, the virtue may still be acquired, although with greater effort. Eight Chapters, Ch. VIII, pp. 85–6.

56. Based on "You shall love the Lord your God with all your heart, with all your soul, and with all your might" (Deuteronomy 6:15), Maimonides states that all human actions should be performed out of love of God. He cites Bar Kappara's famous dictum: Which small section of the Torah incorporates all its principles? that is, "In all your ways acknowledge Him . . ." (Proverbs 3:6), and according to Rabba, the intent of this verse includes even the case of committing a transgression (Berachoth 63a). Maimonides explains this to mean that we cannot condemn an apparent transgression so long as its ultimate purpose is directed to establishing the truth. The ends, however, justify the means only insofar as ceremonial laws are concerned, e.g., violating the Sabbath or eating food on the Day of Atonement in order to preserve life. Eight Chapters, Ch. V, pp. 73–4, and n. 4.

57. The Commentary, Berachoth 4:4, p. 113.

58. Jeremiah 1:12.

59. Proverbs 8:34. This paragraph is deleted, Kapah, p. 280, n. 51.

60. With reference to the gentile, "apikoros–heretic," is translated "atheist." Idolatry does not necessarily deny the existence of a supreme being; some of its forms may be considered misdirected worship, see M.T., Hilchoth Abodath Kochabim 1:1, 2:1.

61. Sanhedrin 38b.

62. Proverbs 2:19. Maimonides understands "apikoros—heretic" as being an Aramaic word which means "mafkir—one who removes restraints." The Commentary, Sanhedrin 10:1, p. 247.

63. The World To Come is represented as the state of the eternal existence of the soul as a disembodied intelligence. Since this state cannot be perceived through the bodily senses, we cannot fathom its nature. In support of our inability to perceive The World To Come, Maimonides cites the Talmudic interpretation of ". . . the eye has not seen a God other than Thee who works for him who waits for Him" (Isaiah 64:13);

in explanation of this it was said: All the prophets prophesied only with regard to The Messianic Era, however, with reference to The World To Come, ". . . the eye has not seen a God other than Thee . . ." (Berachoth 34b, Sanhedrin 99a), The Commentary, Sanhedrin 10:1, p. 246. Apparently, Maimonides differentiates between The World To Come and The Messianic Era. We shall note the relationship between these two states as explained by Maimonides.

In his "Treatise On the Revivification of The Dead," Maimonides explains that the doctrine of The Revivification of The Dead is Torahitic, and it consists of the actual return of the soul to the body, and that the life of The World To Come is a state of existence subsequent to the bodily revivification of the dead, see "Ma'amar T'ḥiyath HaMethim," Lichtenberg, A. L., op. cit., Part II, p. 8d. Thus, the period of revivification is an intermediate state termed The Messianic Era, and it serves as a prelude to the eternal life of The World To Come. The eternal existence of the soul as a disembodied intelligence in The World To Come is merited through the means afforded by The Messianic Era. The latter period is marked by world peace and the cessation of Israel's subjugation to foreign powers. During this finite period, the revivified body, conjoined to its soul, will have the opportunity to study Torah uninterruptedly. At the close of The Messianic Era the revivified bodies will be consumed, and the souls of those who merit it will enter the eternal period of The World To Come, see M.T., Hilchoth T'shubah 9:1, 2; Hilchoth M'lachim 12:1, 2, 4.

1. Psalms 1:2. The following sentence should appear at the beginning of the paragraph: That is to say, were it not for the fear of the kingdom, we would swallow each other alive. Kapaḥ notes that it was added by Maimonides in a later edition of The Commentary, p. 281, and n. 1.

2. Berachoth 6a.

3. Exodus 20:21.

4. This entire paragraph is deleted, Kapaḥ, p. 281, n. 3.

5. I Kings 19:12.

6. Leviticus 10:3. Kapaḥ reads, "v'shabaḥ aharon—and Aaron gave praise." He notes that Maimonides undoubtedly had a different text of the Targum, p. 281, and n. 5.

7. The text of the Mishnah according to Kapaḥ is as follows: Whence do we obtain that even one who sits and studies is considered as if he had fulfilled the entire Torah? Mishnah II, p. 281.

8. Psalms 106:28: "They joined themselves to Baal Peor (i.e., idolatry), and ate of the sacrifices of the dead (i.e., the offerings brought for the worship of an idol)." The Commentary, Abodah Zarah 3:8, p. 186.

9. Isaiah 28:8 probably refers to "vomit and excrement." "Gilulim—idols" (II Kings 23:24), to be understood as "dung"; cp. "gelalay adam—man's dung" (Ezekiel 4:15).

10. "This verse" refers to Isaiah 28:8.

11. Isaiah 28:7–8. "Makom," literally, "space"; figuratively, "Omnipresent." Thus, "b'li makom—with no space," is an allusion to eating and drinking to the exclusion of Torah and its study. The latter part of the Mishnah refers to those who

while at table discuss words of the Torah, and they are considered as if they had eaten of the table of the Omnipresent.

12. Kapaḥ adds the following: Ḥanina ben Ḥachinai said that one who awakens from his sleep at night, and walks in solitude on the road while contemplating denial of religion, warrants punishment from the Lord, p. 282.

13. "Z'man—fortune," meaning life's destiny, or the burden of everyday cares.

14. The eighth of the Thirteen Divine Attributes is that the Torah was Divinely revealed, The Commentary, Sanhedrin 10:1, p. 247. Cp. "He who casts off the yoke of the Torah is one who says, 'The Torah is Divinely revealed but I refuse to bear it,'" Palestinian Talmud, Peah 1:1, p. 16a. Kapaḥ reads, ". . . the Torah is Divinely revealed but I refuse to bear it." In the preceding sentence, after the words, "will deliver him," he adds, "from the yoke of kings and lighten the burden of fortune for him," p. 282.

15. Erubin 54a, with reference to Exodus 32:16.

16. "Elohim—judges," literally, "gods." The Commentary, Sanhedrin 1:1, 6, p. 242.

17. "If he smote him with his hand while it was clenched ("agudah"), M.T., Hilchoth Ḥovel U'Mazik 3:9.

18. Moral virtues result from habit. Intellectual virtue is produced by teaching, *Nicomachean Ethics*, G.B., Vol. IX, Book II, Ch. I, p. 348; cp. infra, pp. 57–8.

19. The text reads "de'oth—acquired knowledge," it should read "ra'oth—evil traits." It apparently is a scribal error, Kapaḥ, p. 283.

20. That is, he dies and does not merit the life of The World To Come. In order to merit the life of The World To Come one must acquire virtues and perfect one's self in this world, for after death this cannot be achieved, infra, Ch. IV, pp. 85–6.

21. Numbers 15:30.

22. Palestinian Talmud, Peah 1:1, p. 16a, with reference to II Kings 23:37.

23. "Literally" may refer to one who draws, or extends the skin in order to conceal circumcision. Cp. One who abrogates the covenant is one who draws the skin, Palestinian Talmud, loc. cit. However, Kapaḥ reads, "'Abrogates the covenant'

refers to one who draws the skin, meaning, he who did not affect circumcision in his adulthood if he was not circumcised by others in his childhood," p. 283. Cp. supra, Ch. II, n. 16.

24. Palestinian Talmud, loc. cit.

25. If he repented of his transgression, and nothing can stand opposed to the repentant, then he should not lose his share in The World To Come!

26. Death incorporates chastisement for ordinary sins and it therefore constitutes an atonement. His sins being atoned for by his death, the ordinary sinner does not lose his share in The World To Come. If a sin mentioned in this Mishnah was atoned for by the sinner, he would not lose his share in The World To Come. In his case, however, due to the severity of his sin, if he did not repent of it during his lifetime, his death would not atone for it and he would lose his share in The World To Come. See M.T., Hilchoth T'shubah 1:4; 3:11.

27. The sense of "kal—plain," not invested with great importance, modest in its significance, as in, ". . . it is too light a thing ("nakel") that you should be My servant . . . ," Isaiah 49:6.

28. The discussion of the manner one to be adopted in approaching sages, supra, Ch. II, pp. 39–40.

29. The word for "youth" in the Mishnah is "tishḥoreth," from "shaḥar—dark," as at dawn; cp. "shaḥarith," meaning "morning," or early period.

30. Supra, Ch. I, Mishnah XV.

31. Since the word "m'kabel" could also be translated "receive," we are informed that Maimonides understands it to mean "greet"—actively, rather than "receive," which has the connotation of passivity. "Makbilloth halula'oth—the loops shall be opposite" (Exodus 26:5), is understood to mean that the loops are engaged through a coupling action in which they go forward to "greet" each other. The Targum translation "l'kibley" for "l'negdo—opposite him" (Joshua 5:13), conveys the meaning "standing so as to greet him." Similarly, the Targum translation "l'kibliḥ for "nochaḥ—before" (Lamentations 2:19), conveys the meaning "greeting the presence of the Lord."

32. This paragraph is deleted, Kapaḥ, p. 284, n. 32.

33. Cp. the "separateness" from the community as an act of virtue, supra, Ch. II, n. 54.

34. M. Ḥagigah 2:7. The Pharisee strictly observed the ritual laws regarding defilement ("tum'ah") and purity ("ta'harah"). The Am Ha'aretz was lax in observing these regulations. ". . . clothes . . . treading-contact defilement": If a leper, or one suffering from a flux (Leviticus 14:1f; 15:1f), were to touch, sit, lie, or lean on a garment, that garment, as well as anyone who subsequently touched it, would become defiled. Therefore, a Pharisee being desirous of maintaining his strict ritual purity, would not as much as come into contact with the clothes of an Am Ha'aretz, since the latter, being lax, might have been in a state of defilement; this constituted the Pharisee's "fence," or "hedge."

35. The reference is to the Eight Chapters, cf. supra, Ch. II, ns. 22, 25.

36. Ibid. A person is responsible for his actions, *Nicomachean Ethics*, G.B., Vol. IX, Book III, Ch. V, pp. 359–61.

37. Exodus 34:6.

38. Erubin 22a.

39. Psalms 145:9.

40. In discussing the subject of repentance, Maimonides states that a man is to be considered either righteous or wicked depending on the balance of his deeds. However, the balance is determined not by the number of deeds, but by their magnitude: "There may be a meritorious deed which balances numerous iniquitous deeds . . . . There may be an iniquitous deed which balances numerous meritorious deeds. These can be balanced only through the knowledge of the omniscient God. He alone knows the valuation of meritorious deeds against iniquitous deeds," M.T., Hilchoth T'shubah 3:2. Where The Commentary reads, "according to the multitude of the deed, not, however, according to the magnitude of the deed," Maimonides is referring to the development of character traits. Thus, with regard to repentance, the magnitude of the deed is significant, and with regard to a man's conditioning himself to the performance of the good, manifold repetition, i.e., the number of deeds, is significant. Eight Chapters, Ch. IV, pp. 58–60.

41. Supra, p. 57.

42. For an analysis of the Platonic "idea" and the Aristotelian "form," see Russell, B., *A History of Western Philosophy*, N.Y., 1965, pp. 119–32, 159–72.

43. Supra, p. 52.

44. This sentence is deleted. The Baraitha of Rabbi Elazar ben Ḥisma was not part of Maimonides' edition of Mishnah Aboth. A later copyist, whose edition contained this Baraitha, appended the first line of The Commentary to Chapter Four to the last line of his Mishnah Aboth Chapter Three. Kapaḥ, p. 285, n. 46.

NOTES TO CHAPTER FOUR

1. One who is content is a rich man. The man of might is one who directs his faculties in accordance with intelligence and reason. Eight Chapters, Ch. VII, p. 80.

2. In discussing The Messianic Era as the period of complete tranquility during which time the revivified dead will have the opportunity to study the Torah and to fulfill its precepts, Maimonides notes with regard to fulfilling the precepts during this period: If one performs but some of the precepts out of love, one is assisted toward fulfilling all of them. However, if one forsakes but one of them out of contempt, one encounters all manner of impediments which prevent the fulfillment of the others. Thus, one's opportunity to merit The World To Come is forfeited. The Commentary, Sanhedrin 10:1, p. 246.

3. Deuteronomy 4:41.

4. Makkoth 10a.

5. Numbers 35:13. The commandment to designate cities of refuge called for six such places. When the tribes of Reuben, Gad, and one-half the tribe of Manasseh, settled in Trans-Jordan prior to the entry of the remainder of the tribes into Canaan (ibid., 32:33f), Moses designated three places to serve as cities of refuge (Deuteronomy 4:41–3); it follows then, that these three places did not become operative as cities of refuge until the remaining three were set aside in Canaan.

6. Although Moses was charged with setting aside six cities of refuge, given the opportunity to fulfill half the commandment, he did so.

7. If Moses was swift to fulfill but part of a precept, how

143

much more should ordinary people who are laden with transgression strive to fulfill a precept!

8. Eight Chapters, Ch. IV, p. 56.

9. "Govah lev—lifted-up of heart" ("arrogant"); "eynayim
ramoth—gaze fixed upwards" ("conceited"); "ruaḥ g'vohah
—lofty spirit" ("insolent"); "gasuth haruaḥ—inflated spirit"
("haughty").

10. Eight Chapters, Ch. IV, pp. 60–1. As a precaution against
a possible tendency toward an extreme, saintly men incline
somewhat toward its opposite extreme, supra, Ch. I, n. 24.

11. So powerful is the attraction of pride and so harmful
are its consequences, that, as a precautionary measure, saintly
men would practice its opposite extreme, namely, humbleness of spirit.

12. Instead of "amongst the bundles of clothes," Kapaḥ reads,
". . . and I was dressed in worn-out rags," p. 287.

13. Supra, n. 11.

14. Modesty is merely a middle course; therefore, humbleness of spirit, being an extreme, is further away from pride, its
opposite extreme, than is modesty. Since the attraction of pride
is so powerful, were a person to rely upon the mean of modesty
he would certainly devolp a bit of pride.

15. Palestinian Talmud, Sabbath 1:3, p. 3b.

16. Psalms 110:10.

17. Proverbs 22:4.

18. The syllogism can be stated as follows: a) fear of the
Lord is greater than wisdom, fear of the Lord being the cause
and wisdom the effect. b) modesty is greater than fear of the
Lord, modesty being the cause and fear of the Lord the effect.
Therefore, modesty is greater than wisdom. The statement that
"fear of the Lord will be found in the train of modesty," is
derived Midrashically from the word "aykev—as a consequence
of" (Proverbs, loc. cit.). Maintaining the same root letters with
a change in vocalization we have "akeyv," meaning "heel,"
i.e., following at the heel of.

19. Megillah 31a.

20. The Torah—from Genesis through Deuteronomy; The
Prophets—from Joshua through Malachi; The Hagiographa—
from Proverbs through II Chronicles.

21. Deuteronomy 10:17.

22. Ibid., 10:18.

23. Isaiah 57:15.

24. Ibid.

25. Psalms 68:5.

26. Ibid., 68:6.

27. Moral and intellectual vices cause separation between man and God. Therefore, by eliminating vices and cultivating virtues man draws nearer to God. The state of prophecy is achieved by attaining all the intellectual virtues and most of the moral virtues. Of all the prophets, Moses attained the highest degree of prophecy by perfecting all the intellectual and the moral virtues, Eight Chapters, Ch. VII, pp. 79–84. For the parallel to this see, Pines, S., *The Guide for The Perplexed*, Chicago, 1963; Prophecy is the perfection of the moral and the intellectual virtues, and given the proper intellectual endowment, perfection can only be achieved through training and development, Part II, Ch. 32, pp. 360–3; Prophecy represents the ultimate form of perfection of the human species, Part II, Ch. 36, pp. 369–73; The distinction of Moses' prophecy, Part II, Ch. 45, pp. 395–403. The attainment of prophecy is the sixth, and the uniqueness of Moses' prophecy is the seventh of the Thirteenth Divine Attributes, The Commentary, Sanhedrin 10:1, p. 247. Cp. The description of "the man of God," infra, Ch. V, pp. 112–14.

According to Professor Abraham J. Heschel, there is little doubt that Maimonides aspired to prophecy. Although Maimonides never explicitly stated this as a goal, he alluded to it in various ways. The attainment of prophecy was important to him. He believed that the power of the intellect is limited, and that prophecy represents the highest type of perception; through it one could apprehend what was beyond the scope of the intellect and thereby resolve questions which otherwise would remain unanswered. In analyzing Joseph ibn Aknin's desire to achieve the state of prophecy, and Maimonides' instructions to him in this regard, and after noting that Maimonides congratulated him on having attained prophecy, Heschel concludes that Maimonides believed that he himself had achieved this state. See Heschel, A. J., "Ha'heh'emin HaRambam Shehzachah Linvuah?," *Louis Ginzberg Jubilee Volume*, N.Y., 1946, pp. 159–188, esp. pp. 159, 160, 164–71, 176–7.

28. Numbers 12:13.

29. That is, he inclined toward the extreme of humbleness of spirit.

30. Exodus 16:7. In a letter to Joseph ibn Aknin Maimonides wrote, "Know, that I strive to act with humility in all matters, even if by so doing it will cause me great harm in the sight of men." *Iggroth HaRambam*, Baneth, D.Z., ed., Jerusalem, 1943, p. 87.

31. Numbers 24:17.

32. M.T., Hilchoth M'lachim 11:1.

33. II Samuel 23:8. "Yosheb bashebeth" means that King David conducted himself with modesty at the academy, Mo'ed Katan 16b.

34. Psalms 51:19.

35. Kapaḥ notes that instead of "ma'aloth—virtues," the text should read "miloth—sayings," p. 287, n. 31.

36. Sotah 4b.

37. Proverbs 16:5.

38. Deuteronomy 7:26.

39. Sotah, loc. cit. The fundamental principle, cf. supra, Ch. I, n. 10.

40. Deuteronomy 8:14.

41. Sotah, loc. cit.

42. Proverbs, loc. cit.

43. Leviticus 18:27. "To'ayvoth ha'el—these abominations," is understood as "abominations to 'El—God'."

44. Sotah, loc. cit.

45. Isaiah 2:22.

46. "a breath," equated with "lofty spirit" ("Insolent").

47. Isaiah, loc. cit.

48. That is, the insolent person is equated with an object of idolatry.

49. Sotah 5a.

50. Isaiah 11:33.

51. Deuteronomy 7:5.

52. Supra, Ch. II, n. 63.

53. Sotah, loc. cit.

54. Isaiah 26:19.

55. Sotah, loc. cit.

56. Psalms 138:6.

57. "Said Rabbi Ashi, every man who has haughtiness in the end will be diminished ("nifḥath")," Sotah, loc. cit., with reference to Leviticus 14:56. This hardly coincides with "sapaḥath —a scab," i.e., a leprous condition. Kapaḥ cites a manuscript of a Midrash which reads, ". . . will eventually suffer the scab ("nispaḥ")," p. 288, n. 43.

58. Isaiah 2:14.

59. Rabba's statement, Sotah, loc. cit.

60. Rabbi Ḥiyya bar Ashi's statement, Sotah, loc. cit.

61. Supra, n. 11.

62. If we accept Rabba's argument, namely, that one sixty-fourth part of pride is approved, how can one consider this minute fraction acceptable if it is sufficient to deem the man who has it, "an abomination of the Lord."

63. Sotah, loc. cit.

64. Proverbs 16:5.

65. Leviticus 4:1–2.

66. Ibid., 19:22.

67. The case cited here of the man who cohabits with a bondmaid who is designated for a man is left unspecified as to whether the sin is either a witting or an unwitting transgression (Leviticus 19:20). It has been suggested that the verse, ". . . and he shall be forgiven for the sin which he sinned" (ibid., 19:22), was inadvertently cited by a copyist, and that the correct reference should have been to the verse, ". . . concerning his sin which he sinned and he shall be forgiven" (ibid., 5:10); this verse refers to the unwitting transgressor who bears sin, Kapaḥ, p. 288, n. 47.

68. Since the unwitting transgressor bears sin and is required to bring a guilt-offering as an atonement, one might conclude that he is placed on a par with the witting transgressor.

69. The fact that the transgressor, witting or unwitting, is guilty of profaning the Name, is to be declared publicly, Yoma, 86b.

70. Maimonides' independent viewpoint and his devotion to what he believed the truth to be, are best illustrated through his willingness to adopt positions which differed from those held by earlier authorities. Rarely, if ever, did a Rabbinic authority

dispute previous Gaonic opinions. To Maimonides' thinking their status did not confer any superior significance to their decisions. For his readiness to refute Gaonim on the grounds of logic, see Introduction to The Mishneh Torah, Wilna edition (Rosenkrantz), Vol. I, p. 5. He did not hesitate to overrule the great Isaac Alfasi whom he revered. Maimonides indicated that his opinions differed from Alfasi's in approximately thirty instances, see *Responsa*, Blau, J., ed., Jerusalem, 1960, Vol. II, no. 217, p. 283, and no. 251, p. 459. So too, in the field of medicine, when convinced of the correctness of his opinion, he refused to accept a view which he believed to be in error no matter how great the prestige of its author. In the twenty-fifth chapter of his "Aphorisms," he mentions more than forty errors made by Galen. This was unique since no previous author had either noted these errors or had the courage to take issue with Galen, see Feldman, W. M., "Maimonides as Physician and Scientist," in *Maimonides,* Epstein, I., ed., London, 1935, pp. 110–11.

71. Instead of ". . . a spade with which to dig," R. T. Herford reads, ". . . a dish wherewith to eat," see *Pirke Aboth,* N.Y., 1925, p. 101, par. 7.

72. Supra, Ch. II, n. 7.

73. The investing authority of a provincial law-court received various emoluments from the local jurisdiction. When The Commentary was first published in 1168, Samuel ben Ali, the Gaon of the Pumbeditha Academy at Baghdad, was in competition with Daniel ben Ḥisda, the Exilarch at Baghdad, for local spheres of influence. This competition continued for more than a score of years and it encompassed the reigns of Daniel ben Ḥisda and his successor, Samuel of Mosul. Contention between the Gaonate and the Exilarchate over numerous issues began more than three and one-half centuries earlier, S. and R., Vol. V, p. 20f.

74. Hillel toiled as a hired man for one-half dinar per day. He paid half his earnings as tuition and the remainder served to support himself as well as the members of his household, Yoma 35b.

75. Sukkah 28a.

76. Berachoth 17b.

77. Sanhedrin 17b.

78. Kethuboth 105a. In either case he did not seek compensation for his services rendered as judge. He merely requested reimbursement for the loss he would sustain by not working at his trade.

79. Numbers 15:31. Thus, to cause the Torah to be regarded as just another trade constitutes profanation of the Name. The preceding verse (ibid., 15:30) refers to the person who highhandedly blasphemes the Lord. According to v. 31, this act necessitates the punishment of Extirpation, and as we have seen, Extirpation means forfeiture of the life of The World To Come, supra, Ch. II, n. 7.

80. Rabbi Elazar, the son of Rabbi Simeon, upon receiving a gift which he accepted, applied to himself, "She is like the merchant ships . . . ," Baba Metzia 84b with reference to Proverbs 31:14. According to Maimonides, those who distorted the meaning of such incidents in order to justify their acceptance of gifts, interpreted this story to mean that, like Rabbi Elazar, they too may accept donatives.

81. At the time Rabbi Elazar saw fit to accept this gift he was physically incapable of performing work, Baba Metzia, loc. cit.

82. Said with regard to Rabbi Shesheth, Gittin 67b.

83. The virtue of contentedness, supra, n. 1.

84. Berachoth 10b. Instead of "simpletons," the text reads "confused madmen," Kapaḥ, p. 290, n. 70.

85. II Kings 4:8f.

86. Berachoth, loc. cit.

87. That is, a scholar has the option of following either the practice of Elisha or that of Samuel. He may choose to follow the practice of Elisha provided there be a sufficient reason for accepting hospitality. To follow the practice of Samuel would mean not to accept hospitality even where sufficient reason existed.

88. Pesaḥim 49a. That is, he pays no heed to the admonition that there be sufficient reason before he chooses to accept hospitality. The result of such action: In the end he causes his house to be destroyed, widows his wife, orphans his young, forgets what he learned, many disputes come upon him, his words are not obeyed, and he profanes the Name of Heaven,

the name of his teacher, and the name of his father, and he brings an evil name upon himself, his children, and his children's children until the end of all generations.

89. Pesaḥim, loc. cit. Such as the meal associated with a betrothal (Kethuboth 8a), or the redemption of a first-born son (Baba Kamma 80a).

90. Nedarim 62a.

91. If the sages consider Rabbi Tarfon guilty of making use of the Torah in order to save his life, how much more are men of the Torah guilty if they use it to obtain money!

92. Instead of "Rabbenu HaKaddosh," the Talmud reads, "Rabbi [Judah HaNasi]." He said, ". . . let those enter who have studied either Bible, Mishnah, Gemara, Halachah, or Aggadah, but no Am Ha'aretz may enter," Baba Bathra 8a.

93. "Talmid Ḥacham—a disciple of the wise," that is, a learned Pharisee.

94. "Am Ha'aretz," supra, Ch. III, n. 34. The antipathy between the Pharisee and the Am Ha'aretz was mutual. Rabbi Akiba, one of the greatest of the Pharisees, was an illiterate Am Ha'aretz until the age of forty, ARN, Rec. A, Ch. 6, p. 28. After he became a Pharisee, he confessed that while he was an Am Ha'aretz his feelings were as follows: Would that I were given a Talmid Ḥacham, I would bite him as does a donkey, Pesaḥim 49b.

95. Jonathan ben Amram adhered to the principle of not making use of the Torah for the purpose of worldly gain even where it meant deceiving his teacher. Rabbi Tarfon was considered guilty of making use of the Torah in an instance where it meant saving his life. How can one then possibly argue that either a student or scholar is permitted to accept, much less request, payment for his knowledge of the Torah!

Throughout his many years of service as a communal leader of Egyptian Jewry, Maimonides never accepted compensation for any of his endeavors. Professor Salo W. Baron points out that his strict view on this matter was largely academic in his own lifetime. Judges, Synagogue officials, and the like, all received reimbursement for their services, see *The Jewish Community*, Phila., 1948, Vol. I, pp. 181–2. It cannot be denied that Maimonides severely criticized the practice. However, it appears that his outspokenness was directed not so much against the practice itself, but against the blatant deceit on the part of those who did violence to plain and obvious Rabbinic teachings on the subject in order to justify their action.

96. Berachoth 34b.

97. "Whoever who casts merchandise to the scholar's account will merit attendance at the Academy on High," Pesaḥim 53b.

98. The law grants the scholar the right of first sale, not the right of first purchase. "Hold the market for him" (Baba Bathra 22a), means "that none other than he may sell" (Rashi, ad loc.). Instead of "shehyiknu—they should sell [to them]," Kapaḥ suggests that we read, "shehyitnu—they should give [them the beginning of the market]," p. 291, n. 8.

99. That is, there is no Biblical reference. The law merely permits the scholar to accept these gestures if they are extended to him.

100. These are Biblically prescribed, Numbers 18:21-4.

101. Merchants extended such privileges to a respected ignoramus; certainly they could do as much for a scholar.

102. Moslem governments imposed various taxes on Jews, however, these were not paid directly to the government, but to the Jewish community which was responsible for their collection. The community could exempt one of its members from payment of taxes. See Baron, S. W., op. cit., Vol. I, p. 159.

103. Joseph ibn Megas ruled that a scholar is not required to pay taxes, *Ḥiddushim*, Baba Bathra 8a. Maimonides was directly influenced by Ibn Megas, his father's teacher. He indicated that he had in his possession a notebook kept by his father from the latter's student days under Ibn Megas, see Blau, J. op. cit., Jerusalem, 1957, Vol. I, no. 126, pp. 223-8. For the great esteem Maimonides had for Ibn Megas, see Introduction to The Commentary, fol. Berachoth, p. 110.

104. The half-shekel due as a poll tax, Exodus 30:12-14; The Commentary, Sh'kallim 1:4, p. 44.

105. All civil cases, except those involving theft or bodily injury, may be adjudicated either by three non-expert judges or by one judge who is a publicly acknowledged expert. Cases that involve theft or bodily injury require three judges who are publicly acknowledged experts, The Commentary, Sanhedrin 1:1, p. 242. Consequently, Rabbi Ishmael's cautioning against

judging alone is not based on a specific prohibition. He merely disapproves of the practice from the standpoint of ethics.

106. "Fortune," supra, Ch. III, n. 13.

107. Supra, p. 65.

108. The many matters which cause neglect of study will not burden one who is engaged in the Torah. However, if one does not engage in the Torah, he will be preoccupied with these matters and he will not have the opportunity to study.

109. Priesthood, Numbers 25:13; Kingship, II Samuel 22:51.

110. Yoma 72b.

111. Proverbs 8:15-6. "By me" refers to Wisdom, i.e., the Torah.

112. Our text of the Mishnah does not enumerate a Mishnah XV. According to this enumeration of the Mishnayoth, the statement of Rabbi Mattithiah ben Ḥeresh should be Mishnah XV. Other editions of Mishnah Aboth enumerate the statement of Rabbi Judah as Mishnah XIII, cf. our text of Mishnah XII. Thus, the statement of Rabbi Nehorai would be Mishnah XIV, and that of Rabbi Jannai, Mishnah XV. See *Mishnayoth*, Ḥoreb edition, Berlin, 1923, Sect. III, p. 191.

113. The Commentary, Sanhedrin 4:4, p. 243, cp. Sanhedrin 37a. The principle, "In matters of sanctity . . . ," Berachoth 28a. The Great Beth-Din, or Great Sanhedrin, was comprised of seventy-one judges. The chief of the court was termed "Nasi," and the second-ranking member was termed "Ab Beth-Din." The position of the names of the pairs of teachers beginning with Jose ben Joezer and Jose ben Joḥanan refers to these offices respectively, supra, Ch. I, p. 5f. The Great Beth-Din convened in the Hall of Hewn-Stone located in the Temple. Its jurisdiction generally encompassed matters of religion and ritual. The Beth-Din of Twenty-Three, or Small Sanhedrin, were courts of local jurisdiction and were comprised of twenty-three members. These courts were empowered to try cases involving capital offenses, see Blackman, P., *Mishnayoth*, N.Y., 1963, Vol. IV, pp. 233-4.

When a vacancy occured in the Great Beth-Din, each member beneath the rank of the vacant seat advanced one place, and the seventy-first seat was then occupied by a head of a Beth-Din of Twenty-Three. Thus, "In matters of sanctity we elevate" refers to "a head to foxes," meaning, a head of a Beth-

Din of Twenty-Three becomes "a tail," that is, the seventy-first member, "to lions," that is, the Great Beth-Din.

114. The Commentary, Sanhedrin 10:1, p. 246.

115. Ecclesiastes 9:10. The authorship of Ecclesiastes is attributed to Solomon, Sabbath 30a.

116. "It" refers to the short span of time in this world. "An eternal forfeiture," that is, since it is only during man's life-span in this world that he may perfect himself and increase his virtues, after he departs he will no longer have this opportunity.

117. The multitude is of the opinion that: a) the former group which adopts the view that after death there is no further opportunity to perfect one's self and to increase virtues, forfeits this world by abstaining from sensual matters; b) the latter group which adopts the view that after death there is further opportunity to perfect one's self and to increase virtues, gains this world by pursuing sensual matters.

118. Isaiah 5:20.

119. Ecclesiastes 9:10.

120. This sentence is deleted, Kapaḥ, p. 293, n. 12.

121. That is, Samuel the Younger cited Proverbs 24:17-8 for a twofold purpose.

122. All the dead will be revivified in The Messianic Era. At the close of this period their bodies will be consumed and judgment will then take place as to who shall merit the eternal life of The World To Come, supra, Ch. II, n. 63.

123. Deuteronomy 10:17.

124. Sifre Deuteronomy (Om edition, N.Y., 1948) Ha'azinu, Ch. 307, Instead of "we," read, "they," Kapaḥ, p. 294.

125. In saying "hear now, you rebels . . ." (Numbers 20:10), Moses departed from the virtue of forbearance toward the extreme of anger, Eight Chapters, Ch. IV, pp. 67-8.

126. Esau clothed himself with fine raiment before rendering service to his father, Deuteronomy Rabbah 1:14, Vol. II, p. 139a. While serving as scribe to Baladan, Nebuchadnezzar wrote to Hezekiah at the time of the latter's illness. He concluded the letter, "Peace to the great God, peace to Jerusalem, peace to King Hezekiah," Sanhedrin 96a.

127. Berachoth 33b.

128. Eight Chapters, Ch. VIII, p. 89.

1. Rosh Hashanah 32a. Genesis 1:1, 3, 6, 9, 11, 14, 20, 24, 26, 2:18.

2. Cp. Eight Chapters, Ch. VIII, pp. 88–9; supra, Ch. III, p. 59.

3. The purpose of all things in the order of creation is to enable the existence of man, and the ultimate purpose of man is to apprehend the intellectual idea and to attain subjective knowledge, Introduction to The Commentary, fol. Berachoth p. 109.

4. The generations from Adam to Noah: Genesis 5:3, 6, 9, 12, 15, 18, 21, 25, 30, 32. From Noah to Abraham: ibid., 10:1; 11:10, 12, 14, 16, 18, 20, 22, 24, 26.

5. The Mishnah Aboth serves a twofold purpose: a) To demonstrate the validity of the oral tradition as having been given to Moses at Sinai, and that it was transmitted to succeeding generations of its authentic interpreters. b) To record the ethical and moral teachings of the sages in order to learn moral attributes from them, Introduction to The Commentary, fol. Berachoth, p. 108.

6. Genesis 12:1.

7. Ibid., 12:2.

8. Ibid., 12:10. Abraham heeded the command to leave his homeland and to journey to a strange land. The Lord had promised him that in the land of Canaan he would be made into a great nation, instead, he encountered a famine which compelled him to depart for Egypt.

9. Ibid., 12:15.

10. Ibid., 14:12.

11. Ibid., 16:2–3; keeping in mind that the Lord had said, ". . . to your seed will I give this land . . ." ibid., 12:7.

12. Ibid., 17:24.
13. Ibid., 20:2.
14. Ibid., 17:2; 21:10.
15. Ibid., 21:12.
16. Ibid., 21:11.
17. Ibid., 21:12, 14.
18. Ibid., 22:1–2.
19. Exodus 8:14.
20. Source unknown.
21. Exodus 7:21.
22. Ibid., 7:28–9.
23. Ibid., 8:18.
24. Ibid., 9:6.
25. Ibid., 9:11.
26. Ibid., 9:26.
27. Ibid., 10:14.
28. Ibid., 10:23.
29. The plague of the slaying of the first-born was directed solely against the Egyptians, ibid., 11:5.
30. Mechilta (Lauterbach, J.Z., ed., Phila., 1949) Beshallah, Ch. V, Vol. I, pp. 223–4; ARN, Rec. A, Ch. 33, p. 96f.
31. Exodus 14:21.
32. Habakkuk 3:14 is interpreted Midrashically. "Nakavta— You pierced," rather than "You smote." "B'matav— for the sake of his tribes," rather than "with his own rods." "Rosh p'razav—its separated headwaters," rather than "the head of his rulers." Cp. Genesis 2:10, "u'misham yipared v'hayah l'arba'ah rawshim—from there it separated and became four headwaters."
33. Exodus 14:29.
34. Habakkuk 3:15. "Ḥomer" is usually translated as "the foaming," it may also mean mud, or sticky substance.
35. Psalms 136:13.
36. Ibid., 74:13.
37. Ibid.
38. Instead of "an onyx," Kapaḥ reads, "a sapphire." "Ḥesh-chath—darkness of waters" (Psalms 18:12), is apparently a scribal error and the reference should be "ḥashrath—gathering of waters" (II Samuel 22:12), p. 297, ns. 36, 37.

39. Exodus 15:8.
40. Mechilta Beshallaḥ, Ch. VII, Vol. I, p. 251.
41. I Samuel 4:8.
42. Exodus 14:11.
43. Ibid., 15:24.
44. Ibid., 16:3.
45. Ibid., 16:20.
46. Ibid., 16:27.
47. Ibid., 17:2.
48. Ibid., 32:1.
49. Numbers 11:1. Instead of "when it said, 'murmurers,'" Kapaḥ reads, "concerning conceptions of the truth," p. 297.
50. Ibid., 11:4.
51. Ibid., 14:22.
52. The Azarah is the court that faced the entrance to the Sanctuary, The Commentary, Middoth 3, diagrams pp. 78–9. The altar upon which the sacrifices were offered, Exodus 40:29.
53. Pesaḥim 54a. This passage is deleted, Kapaḥ, p. 298, and n. 57.
54. Unlike our sages who believed that all phenomena were instituted into the natural order during the six days of creation, the Mutakallimun believed that the Divine Will periodically ordains new phenomena. Eight Chapters, Ch. VIII, pp. 90–1.
55. They are all equal in their having been instituted into the natural order during the six days of creation.
56. Koraḥ and his company, Numbers 16:32; the well, Exodus 17:6; the donkey, Numbers 22:28; the bow, Genesis 9:13; the manna, Exodus 16:15; the rod, Exodus 17:10; the shamir, Jeremiah 17:1, Ezekiel 3:9, for its description in Rabbinic literature as being an insect capable of cutting hard substances, see infra, pp. 101–2, and n. 63; the grave of Moses, Deuteronomy 34:6; the ram of Abraham, Genesis 22:13.
57. Exodus 24:12.
58. Ibid., 32:16.
59. In fashioning each aspect of nature during the six days of creation, the Holy One instituted as a condition of nature that each aspect would bear the specific wonder associated with it, see Genesis Rabbah 5:4, Vol. I, p. 6a. However, the ten wonders cited in this Mishnah were created on the eve of Sabbath at twilight.

60. Instead of "They stated . . . ," Kapaḥ reads, "I will relate to you . . . ," p. 298.

61. The parting of the waters on the second day of creation, Genesis 1:6; the parting of the Red Sea, Exodus 14:21; the parting of the Jordan for Joshua, Joshua 3:16; for Elijah, II Kings 2:8; for Elisha, II Kings 2:14.

62. Joshua 10:12–3.

63. No metal implements were used in preparing the building blocks for the Temple, I Kings 6:7. The shamir was used for cutting the precious stones of the Ephod (Exodus 28:9–11), Gittin 68a.

64. Instead of "He also does not have acquired knowledge ("de'oth")," Kapaḥ reads, "and also before he has acquired evil dispositions ("ra'oth")," p. 298, and n. 77.

65. M. Peah 2:2.

66. There are two reasons why it is impossible to conceive of society without persons who are incapable of intellectual attainment: a) Civilization necessitates many manual services. b) Those who are capable of intellectual attainment are few in number and would be left desolate and alone were it not for the others, Introduction to The Commentary, fol. Berachoth, p. 110.

67. M. Kellim 12:6.

68. Psalms 139:16.

69. Cf. supra, Ch. IV, p. 65, and n. 10. Supra, Ch. III, Mishnah IX.

70. "Ḥesed—a kind act," Genesis 40:14. Its opposite, a decidedly impious act, is euphemistically termed "ḥesed," Leviticus 20:17.

71. In place of "the knowledge," the text reads "the Gemara." Kapaḥ reads, "the Torah, the study, and the practice will be fulfilled." He notes that "the Torah" may be taken to mean "the knowledge," that is, "acquired wisdom," p. 299, and n. 87.

72. The categories of knowledge are distinct, e.g., speculative philosophy is divided into: 1) mathematics, i.e., preliminary discipline, 2) physics, 3) metaphysics. See Friedlander, M., *The Guide of The Perplexed*, Introduction, p. 3, n. 2.

73. Concerning demonstrative knowledge: "It follows that we cannot in demonstrating pass from one genus to another. We

cannot, for instance, prove geometrical truths by arithmetic
. . . Nor can the theorem of any science be demonstrated by
means of another science," *Posterior Analytics*, G.B., Vol. VIII,
Book I, Ch. VII, p. 103. Aristotle's four causes: the material,
the formal, the efficient, and the final, see *Metaphysics*, G.B.,
Vol. VIII, Book V, Ch. II, pp. 533-4.

74. Supra, p. 103.

75. Deuteronomy 28:23.

76. The clear intent of the sages is to prevent delay in rendering decision, see M. Sanhedrin 4:1. The decision is not to
be postponed, yet it must not be rendered hastily, supra, Ch. I,
p. 2.

77. In every year the first tithe was given to the Levite and
the second tithe was to be eaten in Jerusalem. If the distance
was too great, one could convert the second tithe into money
and spend that sum in Jerusalem on edibles. In the third and
the sixth years the second tithe was set aside for the poor. See
Numbers 18:21-6; Deuteronomy 14:22-9.

78. Gleanings, Leviticus 19:9; forgotten sheaf, Deuteronomy
24:19; corner of the field, Leviticus loc. cit.; fallen fruit and
gleanings of the vineyard, Leviticus 19:10.

79. Exodus 23:16, 34:32; Leviticus 23:39.

80. Therefore, pestilence increases in retribution for not setting aside the gifts prescribed to the poor.

81. Supra, Ch. I, ns. 16, 24.

82. That is, toward the extreme opposite to the one taken by
the saintly man, Eight Chapters, Ch. IV, pp. 55-8; 60-1.

83. Accordingly, one who practices the virtue of forbearance which is the mean between the extremes of anger and
insensibility to disgrace, is termed "a wise man." One who
does not follow the precise mean, but prevents the possibility of being angered by inclining toward its opposite extreme, is termed "a saintly man," M.T., Hilchoth De'oth 1:4-5.
For the incident of the saintly man who practiced the extreme
of insensibility to disgrace, see supra, Ch. IV, pp. 65-6.

84. Intellectual virtue has its seat in the Rational Faculty, cf.
supra, Ch. II, n. 44. It is comprised of two categories: 1) Wisdom; 2) Reason. Reason consists of: a) inborn, theoretical reason, that is, fundamental axioms that require no proof and

are explained by common sense; b) the acquired intellect; c) sagacity and intellectual cleverness, that is, the ability to comprehend quickly, Eight Chapters, Ch. II, pp. 49–50.

85. Interestingly, "excessive in mercy" is not defined as a precautionary measure against cruelty.

86. Supra, pp. 103–4.

87. Moderation is the mean between the extremes of excessive passion—the extreme of excess, and insensibility to pleasure—the extreme of deficiency. The extreme of excess is termed "Evil," and the extreme of deficiency is termed "Sin."

88. "Al hanefesh" (Numbers 6:11) means that the Nazirite sinned by suffering defilement through coming into contact with a corpse ("nefesh meth," ibid., v. 6). The sages understand "al hanefesh" to mean that he sinned against the soul, i.e., against himself, for at the conclusion of the period of his vow he is required to bring a sin-offering (ibid., v. 14), Nedarim 10a. That is to say, he is considered a sinner because he refrained from partaking of what is permitted, i.e., he practiced the extreme of insensibility to pleasure, Eight Chapters, Ch. IV, p. 63.

89. For the concluding clause of the sentence the text has, "and who have learned the intellectual." It is obviously corrupt, and it should read as corrected. See Kapaḥ, p. 301, and n. 95.

90. The guilefully wicked is depicted as one who informs the judge of his side of the case before the other litigant arrives at court, Sotah 21b. With reference to ". . . woe to the wicked, it shall be ill with him . . ." ("l'rasha ra," Isaiah 3:11), the sages ask whether there is a case of a wicked man ("rasha") who is evil ("ra"), and a wicked man who is not evil? Yes, one who is evil to God and to man is evilly wicked ("rasha ra"), whereas one who is wicked to God but not to man is merely wicked ("rasha"), Kiddushin 40a.

91. Jeremiah 4:22.

92. *Nicomachean Ethics*, G.B, Vol. IX, Book VII, Ch. I, p. 395.

93. Maimonides' father wrote a commentary to Psalm 90 in which he explained that the words, "A prayer of Moses the man of God. . . ," mean that Moses was unique among the prophets. Nevertheless, every prophet who resembled him by possessing one or more of his characteristics was termed "the

man of God." See Simmons, A. L., "The Letter of Consolation of Maimun ben Joseph," *The Jewish Quarterly Review* (O.S.) Vol. II, p. 87.

94. Judges 2:1. "Malach—messenger," rather than "angel," see Pines, S., *The Guide for The Perplexed*, Part II, Ch. 6, p. 262.

95. "The brutish man," supra, n. 92.

96. Proverbs 17:2. That is, he is a combination of the intellectual and the moral vices.

97. Malachi 2:7.

98. For the prerequisites of prophecy, see supra, Ch. IV, n. 27.

99. The text reads "Seventh Chapter." The purpose of the perfect Torah which guides us to perfection is, to offer instruction in following the course of moral virtue, Eight Chapters, Ch. IV, p. 63.

100. Proverbs 3:17.

101. Eight Chapters, Ch. IV, p. 64.

102. Kapaḥ adds, "All friendship that is dependent on a vain thing, when the thing ceases, the friendship ceases. That which is not dependent on a vain thing will never cease," p. 302. In discussing the three types of friendship, Aristotle states, "The useful is not permanent . . . when the motive of the friendship is done away, the friendship is dissolved," *Nicomachean Ethics*, G.B. Vol. IX, Book VIII, Ch. III, pp. 407–8.

103. Such as the motive of the friendship of the master and disciple who are engaged in the mutual pursuit of the good, supra, Ch. I, pp. 8–9. The good in this case represents the attainment of "genuine knowledge," that is, knowledge of the idea, see the discussion of knowledge and understanding, supra, Ch. III, pp. 60–1.

104. The statement, "For I have hardened his heart and the hearts of his people . . ." (Exodus 10:1), means that God precluded Pharaoh from repentance. If Pharaoh had no choice in the matter, why was he punished? Maimonides resolves this problem as follows: Pharaoh oppressed the children of Israel of his own free will and he also caused his people to sin, viz., "And he said to his people . . . Come let us deal wisely with them . . ." (ibid., 1:9–10). Justice demands that Pharaoh be punished for this, and the retribution that God meted out to him was that He precluded him from repentance. Thus, by being withheld

from the possibility of repentance, Pharaoh inevitably received the punishment that he deserved, Eight Chapters, Ch. VIII, pp. 94–5. See M.T., Hilchoth T'shubah 6:3.

105. For "contentedness," see supra, Ch. II, p. 36. Although "inordinate modesty" is the extreme, it is recommended as the course to follow since "modesty," the mean, cannot effectively counterbalance the attraction of the extreme of pride, supra, Ch. IV, p. 65, and n. 11.

106. Genesis 14:23.

107. Ibid., 12:11; since until that day Abraham did not know that Sarah was beautiful, the Talmud concludes that he had not looked at her, Baba Bathra 16a.

108. Genesis 16:6. Hagar had already conceived, ibid., v. 5.

109. Ibid., 21:11. Instead of ". . . in order that she preclude him from turning to her for sexual relations," Kapaḥ reads, "When Sarah requested him to banish her with Ishmael, Scripture attested that this was difficult for him only as it regarded Ishmael; [Sarah did this] in order to clear him of suspicion that he had an inclination toward her (i.e., Hagar) for sexual relations," p. 303.

110. Genesis 18:27.

111. Deuteronomy 23:5.

112. Numbers 31:16.

113. Literally, "copulated with his donkey," Sanhedrin 105a.

114. Numbers 24:16.

115. Proof is adduced from Psalms 55:24 that Balaam and his disciples will not inherit The World To Come. Balaam fulfilled the qualifications of the verse by being both a man of blood and a man of deceit. He was a man of blood by virtue of the plague which was visited upon Israel because of their harlotry with the women of Moab (Numbers 25:1, 9). He was a man of deceit by virtue of his stratagem for the commission of evil deeds.

116. The proof that the disciples of Abraham will inherit The World To Come is derived from the interpretation of Proverbs 8:21. The letters of the word "yesh—substance," have the numerical value of three hundred ("shin") and ten ("yod"). The "substance" refers to the three hundred and ten worlds that the disciples of Abraham will inherit, see M. Ukt-

zin 3:12. In Isaiah 41:8 Abraham is termed "ohabi—My beloved." Abraham's seed is equated with "ohabaiy—them that love Me" of Proverbs 8:21. Thus, Abraham's seed will "inherit substance."

117. II Samuel 22:27.

118. Yebamoth 79a; Exodus 20:20.

119. His full name, Johanan ben Bag Bag, is cited in Kiddushin 10b. He was either a proselyte or the son of proselytes. The possibility that he was a son of proselytes is derived from "Bag Bag" taken as an acronym from "Ben Ger—Bath Ger," meaning that his father and mother were proselytes. The alternative that he himself was a proselyte is based on the numerical value of the letters "Beth—two," and "Gimel—three," equalling five. The letter for the number five is "He," it being the letter that was added to the names of Abram and Sarai (Genesis 17:1-5, 15), i.e., he was a son of Abraham and Sarah, meaning that he was a proselyte. To a proselyte who questioned Maimonides as to whether he is permitted to recite the words, "Our God and God of our fathers, the God of Abraham . . ." as found in the first benediction of the Eighteen Benedictions, he wrote: "Therefore, everyone who becomes a proselyte, until the end of all generations, as well as everyone who declares the unity of God as written in the Torah (Deuteronomy 6:4), is a disciple of Abraham our father, peace be upon him, . . . Therefore, you may recite "Our God and God of our fathers. . . ," because Abraham, peace be upon him, is your father, . . . inasmuch as you have come under the wings of the Divine Presence and have joined Him, there is no distinction between you and me." *Responsa*, Blau, J., ed., Jerusalem, 1960, Vol. II, no. 293, p. 549.

120. Genesis 18:2, Targum, ad loc.

121. Based on the explanation offered above in n. 119, "Ben He He" and "Ben Bag Bag" might be either one and the same person or two different persons.

122. With reference to Ecclesiastes 2:9: "Rabbi Aḥa said, of all the Torah that I learned, the only part that remained with me was what I acquired through the blows given to me in anger by my teacher," Ecclesiastes Rabbah 2:12, Vol. II, p. 113b.

123. Instead of "mora—awe," the Talmud reads, "marah—bitterness," Kethuboth 103b. This applies only to the slothful student. However, if the student is not gifted, or if the subject matter is difficult, the teacher is required to exhibit patience, see M.T., Hilchoth Talmud Torah 4:5.

The Commentary to Mishnah Aboth ends at this point. The Sixth Chapter of Mishnah Aboth, called "Perek Rabbi Meir," or "Perek Kinyan Torah," was not part of the Mishnah as compiled by Rabbi Judah HaNasi. This chapter was added after the closing of the Babylonian Talmud and is found in the post-Talmudic literature as the eighth chapter of Kallah Rabbathi and as the seventeenth chapter of Tanna de Be Eliahu Zutta, see Herford, R. T., *Pirke Aboth*, N.Y., 1925, Introduction, pp. 11–4. Herford is of the opinion that the original Mishnah Aboth ended with the words, ". . . Father who is in Heaven," as found in Mishnah XX. He considers, "May it be Your will . . ." as a doxology added by a later writer who apparently regarded the preceding sentence as the conclusion of Mishnah Aboth, ibid., p. 144.

Index

Authorities Cited in The Mishnah